HANDBOOK
on the
CONSTITUTIONS
of the
UNITED STATES
and
GEORGIA

HANDBOOK
on the
CONSTITUTIONS
of the
UNITED STATES
and
GEORGIA

MERRITT B. POUND

and

ALBERT B. SAYE

TWELFTH EDITION

THE UNIVERSITY OF GEORGIA PRESS

ATHENS

The paper in this book meets the guidelines for permanence and durability of the Committee on Production Guidelines for Book Longevity of the Council on Library Resources.

Printed in the United States of America

Library of Congress Cataloging in Publication Data

Pound, Merritt Bloodworth, 1898–
Handbook on the Constitutions of the United States and Georgia.
Bibliography: p.
1. Georgia—Constitutional law. 2. United States—Constitutional law. I. Saye, Albert Berry. II. Title.
KFG402.Z9P6 1984 342.758′023 83-4939
ISBN 0-8203-0692-4 347.580223

First published in 1946

Contents

Foreword
(to first edition)

The General Assembly of Georgia passed the following act in the year 1923:

> . . . all schools and colleges in this State that are sustained or in any manner supported by public funds shall give instruction in the essentials of the United States Constitution and the Constitution of Georgia, including the study of and devotion to American institutions and ideals, and no student in said schools and colleges shall receive a certificate of graduation without previously passing a satisfactory examination upon the provisions and principles of the United States Constitution and the Constitution of the State of Georgia.

For the benefit of students not exempted from this requirement by course credit, the University of Georgia offers examinations over the two Constitutions on the first Thursday after Washington's birthday.

In 1936 Dr. Albert B. Saye prepared a pamphlet in mimeographed form for use in connection with a series of lectures designed to aid students in preparing for these examinations. The original pamphlet entitled *Outline and Questions on the Constitutions of the United States and the State of Georgia*, of which this booklet is an outgrowth, was published in printed form in 1940 and again in 1942.

The adoption by the people of Georgia of the Constitution of 1945 necessitated a revision of the outline and questions on the Constitution of Georgia. It was decided by Dr. Saye, the original author, to expand beyond the outline stage and to include within the expanded booklet the actual texts of the Constitutions of the United States and of Georgia with discussions of the provisions of these documents. The undersigned was invited to collaborate and is responsible for the sections devoted to the Constitution of the United States. The sections applying to the Constitution of Georgia were prepared by Dr. Saye.

This handbook is offered to the students of the University System of Georgia and to the citizens of Georgia with the hope that it will aid them to an intelligent understanding of the constitutional principles under which our national and state governments operate.

MERRITT B. POUND

Athens, Georgia
November, 1945

Preface

TWELFTH EDITION

In the 1984 revision of this *Handbook* only minor changes have been made in Part I relating to the Constitution of the United States. Part II, dealing with the Constitution of Georgia, has been revised extensively to reflect the changes made by the adoption of the Constitution of 1983.

As in past editions, a full copy of the Constitution of the United States is contained in this edition; but the extreme length of the present Constitution of Georgia makes it cumbersome for a handbook. The document is analyzed here, but not quoted in full. A free copy of the Constitution of Georgia can be obtained by addressing a request therefor to Mr. Max Cleland, Secretary of State, State Capitol, Atlanta, Georgia 30334.

A.B.S.

PART I

The Constitution of the United States

Introduction

HISTORICAL BACKGROUND

Political institutions result from an evolutionary growth. Thus most American political institutions have their origin in the constitutional history of England prior to the 18th Century. The American Revolution did not produce an immediate and drastic change in the forms of local government; it only severed the political tie that bound the colonies to the Mother Country. Separated from England by time and space the American colonists developed self reliance. Gradually social, economic, religious and political differences appeared. It was but natural that the colonies should seek independence.

From the day the Mayflower arrived in Plymouth Bay in 1620 a series of political incidents occurred which became antecedents of modern American government. Even before the Pilgrims had gone ashore they drew up an agreement known as the Mayflower Compact. This marks the beginning of cooperative political action on the part of individual English colonists in the New World. In 1639 the river towns of the Connecticut Valley drew up the Fundamental Orders of Connecticut, the first written constitution in history by which a government came into existence. In 1641 the Massachusetts Body of Liberties became the first law code drawn up on North American soil. The four New England colonies in 1643 formed a cooperative agreement among themselves called the New England Confederation for protection from the Indians. It was the first cooperative agreement between colonies. In 1754 an attempt was made at Albany to draw all of the colonies into a closer union and Benjamin Franklin presented a plan of union which was rejected. After the treaty of peace ending the French and Indian War (1763) England changed her commercial policy. A stamp tax, levied on several commodities, aroused bitter opposition in the colonies and a Stamp Act Congress was assembled to protest this tax. The stamp tax was repealed but events were rapidly leading to the break. In 1774 all of the colonies except Georgia sent representatives to the First Continental Congress. Again protests against grievances were sent to the English crown.

In 1775 there assembled in Philadelphia representatives of all the colonies in the Second Continental Congress. Though this Congress had no legal basis it became a *de facto* government and the first national government of the United States. By the Declaration of Independence (1776) it proclaimed the thirteen colonies independent of English control and proceeded to raise an army, appoint a commander-in-chief, borrow money and negotiate treaties—things only a government can do. The common stress of the times made the *de facto* system of government work, but it was realized that it could be only a temporary expedient.

ARTICLES OF CONFEDERATION

On June 7, 1776, simultaneously with his resolution of independence, Richard Henry Lee offered a resolution in the Continental Congress to form a confederation. His resolution was adopted on June 11 and a committee was appointed to prepare a plan. The Articles of Confederation were adopted by Congress on November 15, 1777, but they provided for unanimous state acceptance and were not ratified by Maryland, the last state to agree, until March 1, 1781.

The Articles of Confederation established the first *de jure* national government and became the first written constitution of the United States. This constitution served from March 2, 1781, until the present constitution was ratified and became effective in 1789. There were thirteen articles and, as the title implies, they created a confederate government. Article I stated: "The title of this Confederacy shall be 'The United States of America'." Article II left no doubt as to the nature of the new government. "Each State retains its sovereignty, freedom and independence. . . . " In the preamble the new constitution was called "Articles of Confederation and perpetual Union," but Article III weakened this definition somewhat by the statement that the states had entered "a firm league of friendship with each other...."

Article IV contained several provisions which were carried over almost verbatim into the present constitution. "Free inhabitants of each of these States . . . shall be entitled to all privileges and immunities of free citizens in the several States. . . ." It also provided for rendition of fugitives and ended with the following clause: "Full faith and credit shall be given in each of these States to the records, acts and judicial proceedings of the courts and magistrates of every other State."

Article V provided for a Congress of one chamber to be composed of from two to seven delegates from each state annually appointed. Regardless of the number of delegates a state decided to send to Congress each state had only one vote.

Article VI imposed limitations upon the states. There were to be no treaties without the consent of Congress or interference with treaties entered into by the United States. No vessels of war should be kept in time of peace except as Congress approved, nor should any state engage in war without this consent.

Article VII placed the land forces under the states with the right of each state to appoint all officers within its forces up to and including the rank of colonel. Though Article IX conferred on Congress the sole and exclusive right of determining on war and peace, Article VII definitely put the national government in the position of having to rely upon the states for its armed forces.

Article VIII placed upon the states the obligation of contributing to all national expenses in proportion to the land values in each state but gave no power to Congress to collect these obligations, saying, "The taxes for paying that proportion shall be laid and levied by the authority and direction of the Legislatures of the several States. . . ."

Article IX, the longest of the thirteen, enumerated the powers of Congress but no important power was to be exercised "unless nine States assent to the same." Under this limitation legislation was often defeated, even though unopposed, by the absence of delegates.

In Article X a committee of the states was provided for which could exercise such powers in a recess of Congress as Congress saw fit to vest in this committee. However, no powers requiring the votes of the delegates of nine states could thus be exercised.

Article XI was an invitation to Canada to membership in the Confederation.

Article XII recognized all obligations incurred by Congress before the ratification of the Articles as valid debts against the United States.

Article XIII provided that amendments to the Articles must be agreed to in Congress and confirmed by the legislatures of all the states.[1]

Certain defects of the Articles of Confederation are obvious. The absence of a strong national government reflected the jealousy of the states of their recent independence. Serving as the constitution of the United States during the period commonly known as "The critical period in American History" the Articles, nevertheless, had some definite accomplishments. The country was kept united. The peace treaty with England was negotiated and signed. The Northwest Ordinance of 1787, the basis of

1. *Documents Illustrative of the Formation of the Union of the American States.* House Doc. No. 398, 69th Congress, 1st Session (Washington, 1927), 27-37.

territorial regulation to the present day, was adopted, and the antecedents of executive departments were created.

Weaknesses were many. There was a President of the Congress of the United States, but no clearly defined executive department and no national system of courts. The states were completely sovereign and alone had jurisdiction over individuals. Requisitions for money and troops were made on the states. It was government by supplication. Congress could not regulate interstate commerce and the difficulties of amending the Articles were great.

THE FEDERAL CONVENTION

The inability of Congress under the Articles of Confederation to regulate interstate commerce resulted in controversies between the states. Maryland and Virginia were having trouble over navigation on the Potomac River. Maryland claimed that under its original charter the south bank of the river was its southern boundary and placed restrictions on the use of the river by Virginia. Virginia countered by imposing duties on goods entering the Chesapeake bound for Maryland. The two states agreed to discuss these difficulties by conference and five delegates, three from Maryland, two from Virginia, met at Alexandria in 1785. They adjourned to Mount Vernon at Washington's invitation and there reached an amicable agreement. However, it was decided by the delegates that since interstate controversies were also plaguing the other members of the Confederation all of the states should be invited to send delegates to a similar conference at Annapolis in 1786. The legislatures of Virginia and Maryland issued such an invitation. Only five states were represented when this second conference convened, but out of it came the suggestion that all states select delegates to attend a convention in Philadelphia for the purpose of discussing revision of the Articles of Confederation. Among those present at Annapolis were Alexander Hamilton of New York and James Madison of Virginia. The date of the convention was set for May 14, 1787, but it was not until May 25 that a quorum had arrived and the convention began its sessions.

Every state, with the exception of Rhode Island, selected delegates. Only fifty-five actually appeared at any of the sessions though more were designated to attend. Twenty-nine delegates were present at the opening session. The average attendance was about forty. Thirty-nine delegates, representing twelve states, signed the Constitution as it was finally adopted.

Among the prominent delegates who played leading parts in

the deliberations were George Washington, Edmund Randolph and James Madison of Virginia; Benjamin Franklin, James Wilson and Gouverneur Morris of Pennsylvania; Alexander Hamilton of New York; and William Patterson of New Jersey.

On the whole the delegates were property owners and shareholders in the defunct confederate government. Many of them had vested interests in a strong government able to protect property rights and investments. There were few representatives of the small farming and mechanic classes. Of the fifty-five delegates who attended one or more sessions, forty were holders of public securities; fourteen were speculating in lands; and fifteen were slaveholders. Most of the members were experienced in government and many had been members of the Continental Congress. It was a well educated group with at least twenty-four college graduates among its membership. Thirty-one delegates were trained in the law. The membership, on the whole, was young and vigorous, the average age of the members being about forty. There were, however, older statesmen present such as Franklin and Washington. The chaotic conditions of the years following the Revolution had convinced the majority of the members that a strong national government was a necessity.

George Washington, the best known and most highly respected American, was chosen to preside at the convention. Most delegates were instructed only to discuss revision of the Articles of Confederation, but it was early decided to present to the states for approval an entirely new constitution. Meetings of the convention were secret and voting was by states.

The Virginia delegation had prepared its plan of union prior to the opening session of the convention. It was presented by Edmund Randolph and is known as the Randolph, the Virginia, or the Large State Plan. Under this plan the national government was to be greatly strengthened and an entirely new machinery of government was to be established. It called for a national executive, a national tribunal, and a bicameral legislature with proportional representation in each chamber.

The Large State Plan, with its provision for proportional representation in Congress, met with opposition from the delegates of the small states who presented a plan known as the Patterson, the New Jersey, or the Small State Plan. It was presented by William Patterson of New Jersey. By this plan only the glaring defects of the Articles of Confederation were to be corrected. Congress was to remain a unicameral body with equal state representation.

There was a high degree of unanimity among the delegates

that the national government should be strengthened, but compromises were necessary because of the difference in size and the social and economic interests of the various states. The Connecticut delegates presented the compromise between the Large and the Small State Plans. Known at the Connecticut Compromise, or Great Compromise, it called for the present form of Congress, namely, a House of Representatives with representation proportional to population, and a Senate with equal state representation.

Sectional differences were also in evidence. A difference of opinion arose between the northern states and the southern slaveholding states as to the counting of slaves for representation in the House of Representatives. A later decision to apportion direct taxes among the states in proportion to population gave a basis for another compromise. It was decided by the Three-fifths Compromise that three-fifths of the slave population should be counted both for representation and direct taxes.

Lack of control of interstate commerce, it has been pointed out several times, was a glaring defect of the Articles of Confederation. Nevertheless, the southern states were reluctant to give Congress the power to control commerce without some assurance that the slave trade should not be interfered with under this power or southern exports penalized. A compromise gave Congress the broad power to regulate foreign and interstate commerce but denied it the right to place duties on exports or to interfere with the slave trade prior to 1808.

A single elective executive, to be known as the President, was agreed upon, and a federal court system was provided for. Ratification was to be by conventions in the states. Ratification by nine states was necessary to make the new constitution effective.

Thirty-nine delegates representing twelve states signed the completed document on September 17, 1787, each subordinating certain personal opinions to the combined wisdom of the majority of the delegates.

CAMPAIGN FOR RATIFICATION

The campaign for ratification revealed opposition in several key states, namely, Virginia, Pennsylvania, Massachusetts and New York. Among the objections raised were: there was no bill of rights or protection of the individual from the assumption of powers on the part of the nation government; the national government was too strong; or, the national government was too weak. Nevertheless, the friends of ratification proved strongest and eleven states, two more than the necessary minimum, had ratified in convention in time for the election of President Washington and his inauguration on April 30, 1789. Rhode Island and North Carolina alone held out. In New York, where opposition was great, Alexander Hamilton, James Madison and John Jay in a series of published articles signed "Publius" and known collectively as *The Federalist*, or *The Federalist Paper*, were influential in getting the document approved.

FUNDAMENTAL PRINCIPLES OF THE CONSTITUTION

Among the cardinal principles of the Constitution is that of popular sovereignty and limited government. This means that ultimately all government is subject to the will of the people and that the people, acting through their elected representatives, can amend the fundamental law. Specific limitations are placed upon the national government in Article I, Section 9, and in Articles of Amendment I-VIII, XIII, XV, and XIX. Prohibitions are placed upon the states in Article I, Section 10, and in Amendments XIII, XIV, and XIX. Article IV, Section 4, imposes the obligation upon the national government of guaranteeing republican government to the states.

By means of the Constitution a federal government was created. A government of the federal type is one in which there is a distribution of powers in the fundamental law between the national and state governments. The national government is one of delegated powers and the states have reserved and inherent powers. In the United States, in the case of a conflict of powers, the Supreme Court is the final arbiter.

In its designated field the national government is supreme. The Constitution of the United States is the supreme law of the land. Any other law in conflict, national or state, is void. Citizens of the United States are thus bound by the following laws, each of which must conform to all of those above it: the Constitution of the United States, laws and treaties of the United States made in pursuance of the Constitution, state constitutions and state laws. It is the duty of the judiciary to uphold the supreme law.

Under the Articles of Confederation there was no national judiciary and the executive and legislative branches were not separate. One of the principles of the Constitution is the separation of powers. Congress makes the laws, the executive enforces them, the courts interpret them and punish offenders for their violation. Each of these three coordinate branches of the national government is distinct in personnel and officials can hold office in only one branch. In order to prevent either of the three branches from assuming an undue proportion of powers, it is provided that there shall be checks and balances. The President can check Congress by means of his veto; the courts can check Congress by means of judicial review of legislation; Congress can check the courts by its powers of impeachment, and by the same power can check the executive branch; Congress has an additional check on the executive in that the Senate must ratify treaties and confirm appointments; Congress, also, by its right of initiating constitutional amendments, can overcome the effects of judicial decisions.

America's unique contribution to constitutional government is the doctrine of judicial review of legislation. This means that any law passed by a legislative body, either Congress or a state legislature, may be subjected to review and interpretation by the courts. When Congress oversteps its delegated or implied powers, when a state encroaches on the powers of the national government, or when either a state or the national government abrogates guaranteed civil liberties, the federal judiciary may declare the act unconstitutional, invalid and void. Other laws, not necessarily unconstitutional, are also subject to judicial interpretation and subsequently mean what the courts say they mean even if such meaning was not in the intent of the legislative body enacting the law. This power of the judiciary to review and interpret is not specifically stated in the Constitution. The practice, however, was followed in the colonial period of our history. Two early cases involving this principle were *Holmes* vs. *Walton*, decided in the New Jersey courts in 1780, and *Trevett* vs. *Weeden*, a Rhode Island decision of 1786. In the famous case of *Marbury* vs. *Madison* in 1803 the Supreme Court of the United States declared an act of Congress unconstitutional and proclaimed the doctrine of judicial review. In 1810 in the case of *Fletcher* vs. *Peck* an act of the General Assembly of Georgia was declared void, and in 1816 in *Martin* vs. *Hunter's Lessee*, a case appealed from the Virginia courts, the power of the federal courts to review and reverse the decisions of state courts was enunciated.

The Constitution of the United States is brief, simple, and was beautifully worded by the Committee on Style under the chairmanship of Gouverneur Morris of Pennsylvania. It possesses definiteness in principle, yet elasticity in details. Its framers were not primarily interested in theory; consequently there are conspicuous omissions. No bill of rights was originally attached and the question as to the residence of sovereignty in the new federal Union was avoided. A bill of rights, consisting of the first ten amendments, was added in 1791. A bloody civil war decided the

Union to be indestructible. Many Supreme Court decisions have given meaning to obscure and controversial provisions. In addition to the bill of rights, eleven amendments have been added to change the original document.

A distinction should be drawn between the "formal" Constitution and the "real" or "living" Constitution. The formal document is composed of seven articles and twenty-one articles of amendment and may be changed in accordance with the provisions of Article V. The "real" Constitution, however, is said to grow in three other ways, namely, by those acts of Congress which change the structure of our national government, by decisions of the federal courts having a similar effect, and by usage.

Illustrations of growth by statuory amplification are the ten executive departments which have been created by acts of Congress, the present membership of 435 in the House of Representatives, and the establishment of federal courts other than the Supreme Court. The real Constitution has grown by judicial interpretation in many ways. Two illustrations are the doctrine of implied powers announced in the *McCulloch* vs. *Maryland* decision in 1819 and the doctrine of judicial review proclaimed in 1803 in the case of *Marbury* vs. *Madison*. Growth by usage may be illustrated by the development of the party system and the method of nominating presidential candidates.

THE CONSTITUTION AS AN OBJECTIVE DOCUMENT

As originally adopted the Constitution of the United States is a document of a preamble and seven relatively short articles. The preamble states: "We the people of the United States, in order to form a more perfect Union, establish justice, insure domestic tranquility, provide for the common defense, promote the general welfare, and secure the blessings of liberty to ourselves and our posterity, do ordain and establish this Constitution for the United States of America." The preamble states purposes only and does not confer any powers. It is therefore not generally considered subject to judicial interpretation. However, in the preamble to the Articles of Confederation each of the states to make up the Confederacy was enumerated. As any nine states could make the Constitution operative such enumeration in it was impossible. In the period prior to the Civil War when the major political debates were as to the nature of the Union, the meaning of the words "We the people" was often examined. Was the United States a union of sovereign states, or was it a national union of "the people of the United States"? The nationalist view was ultimately triumphant.[2]

ARTICLE I. It is composed of ten sections and is more than half of the total document in length. If titles had been assigned to the articles this would have been most likely designated "The Legislative Department". Section 1 provides for a bicameral Congress consisting of the House of Representatives and the Senate. Section 2 provides for membership in the House of Representatives, how and by whom elected, term of office, qualifications, apportionment among the several states, enumeration of the number of Representatives each state should originally have, method of filling vacancies, the power of choosing officers, and the power of impeachment.

Section 3 describes the Senate, its membership, how and by whom chosen, qualifications, the President of the Senate, his right to vote, other officers and how chosen, and the power to try impeachments. It should be noted that Clause 1 states that Senators shall be chosen by the state legislatures but that direct election by the people has been substituted by Amendment XVII.

Section 4 confers on the states the right to prescribe the times, places and manner of holding elections for Congress but gives Congress the right to alter such regulations. Under this provision Congress has decreed that Congressional elections shall take place on the Tuesday following the first Monday in November of even years and that Representatives shall be elected from Congressional Districts. This section also calls for an annual meeting of Congress on the first Monday in December until a different date is set by law. Amendment XX, ratified in 1933, changed the date of the annual meeting to January 3.

Section 5 deals with the powers of each House over its membership and the rules of legislative procedure.

Section 6 discusses the compensation, privileges and disqualification of members of Congress.

Section 7 confers upon the House of Representatives the right to originate revenue bills, and contains provisions as to orders, concurrent resolutions, and the overriding of a Presidential veto.

Section 8 contains eighteen clauses. The first seventeen are the enumerated powers of Congress. Clause 18 is the "necessary and proper", or "the elastic", clause, a loose construction or liberal interpretation of which by the Supreme Court is the basis of the implied powers of Congress. This doctrine of "implied powers" was first enunciated by the Supreme Court in the

---

2. See *Texas* vs. *White* (1869), 7 Wallace 700.

famous case of *McCulloch* vs. *Maryland* in 1819. It is safe to say that if Congress today were limited to the enumerated powers it could not do a majority of the things it does.

The words "Negro" and "slave" are not to be found in the Constitution though Negro slavery was a recognized institution.

Section 9 prohibits Congress from interfering with the slave trade prior to the year 1808. It further states that the writ of *habeas corpus* shall not be suspended except in case of rebellion or inv[illegible] of attainder nor *ex post facto* law shall [illegible] taxes shall be levied unless apportioned [illegible] basis of population; that no export taxes [illegible] ports shall be uniform; that no money [illegible] the treasury except by legal appropria- [illegible] of nobility shall be granted. Clause 4, [illegible] less apportioned on the basis of popula- [illegible] Amendment XVI which gave Congress [illegible] taxes without apportionment.

[illegible] tations upon the states similar to those [illegible] Section 9 and, in addition, denies to the [illegible] any treaties or alliances, coin money, [illegible] and silver coin legal tender, lay duties [illegible] without the consent of Congress, keep [illegible] of peace.

[illegible] e might be entitled "The Executive De- [illegible] Section 1 for the office of President, [illegible] ected, qualifications, on whom his duties [illegible] al or death, his compensation and oath [illegible] the President is named Commander-in- [illegible] power to require opinions of the heads [illegible]. He is given powers of appointment [illegible] ht to make treaties. Section 3 confers [illegible] mmunicate with Congress, call Congress [illegible] t in case of disagreement between the [illegible] dors, and commission officers of the [illegible] rged with the duty of seeing that the [illegible] ed. He shall be removed on conviction [illegible]

[illegible] icle might naturally be entitled "The [illegible] ction 1 proclaims "The judicial power [illegible] l be vested in one Supreme Court, and [illegible] Congress may from time to time ordain [illegible] rs did not attempt to set up the details [illegible] t left them to the decision of Congress. [illegible] whatever courts Congress has created or shall create shall hold their offices during good behavior and receive a compensation which shall not be diminished during their continuance in office. As a result of the wording of this section all members of the federal judiciary hold their positions for life unless they resign or are convicted on impeachment charges. In addition to the Supreme Court composed of nine justices Congress has established Circuit Courts of Appeal, District Courts, and other special federal courts. Section 2 confers upon the Supreme Court original jurisdiction in all cases involving ambassadors, other public ministers, and consuls, and in cases in which a state is a party. The judicial power shall extend to all cases in law and equity arising under the Constitution, the laws of the United States, or treaties. All trial of crimes, except in cases of impeachment, shall be by jury. Section 3 defines treason and gives Congress the power to declare punishment for this crime.

ARTICLE IV. This article is often called the "Full faith and credit" article, or "Relations between the states." It proclaims in Section 1 that "Full faith and credit shall be given in each state to the public acts, records, and judicial proceedings of every other State." Section 2 provides that citizens of each state shall be accorded all of the privileges and immunities of citizens in all other states and that fugitives from justice shall be delivered to the officers of the state in which the crime was allegedly committed. Section 3 makes provision for the admission of new states. Section 4 outlines some of the obligations of the United States towards the states. Each state shall be guaranteed a republican form of government and shall be protected from invasion and, upon request, from domestic violence.

ARTICLE V. This is an article of only one paragraph and is devoted to the amending process. Two methods of proposal and two methods of ratification are provided, making, in different combinations of proposal and ratification, four possible methods of constitutional amendment. Until the ratification of Amendment XXI in 1933 only one method had been used, namely, proposal by two-thirds of both Houses of Congress and ratification by the legislatures of three-fourths of the states. The Twenty-first Amendment, however, contained within itself the provision that it should be ratified by conventions in three-fourths of the states. Thus, two methods have now been used. A limitation was placed upon amendments to clause 1 and 4 of Article I, Section 9, until the year 1808, and a permanent restriction was placed on any amendment to the Constitution which would deprive any state of its equal suffrage in the Senate without its consent. The issue has not yet arisen but it is quite doubtful that any provision within a constitutional document designed to prohibit amendment could be enforced.

ARTICLE VI. This is sometimes called "The Supreme law of the land" article as the Constitution is so described in it. Debts contracted prior to the adoption of the Constitution are declared valid. This article also requires all federal and state officers to take an oath or affirmation to support the Constitution but declares there shall never be a religious test for holding federal office.

ARTICLE VII. This article, the schedule of ratification, has accomplished its purpose and is no longer operative. "The ratification of the conventions of nine states shall be sufficient for the establishment of this Constitution between the States so ratifying the same." It should be noted that ratification was by conventions in the states called for that purpose and not by either the state legislatures or the people of the states by direct vote.

AMENDMENTS TO THE CONSTITUTION OF THE UNITED STATES

BILL OF RIGHTS. It will be recalled that one of the objections raised to the Constitution was that there were not within it sufficient safeguards against the assumption by the national government of arbitrary power over the individual citizen. Some who were opposed on these grounds were persuaded to support ratification by the promise that an early attempt would be made to amend the Constitution to provide such safeguards. James Madison, who had been elected to the House of Representatives, accordingly proposed a series of amendments in that body during its first session. Seventeen were adopted by the House and twelve of these received the assent of the Senate. Two of them failed of ratification by the legislatures of three-fourths of the states but the remaining ten became effective on November 3, 1791. These first ten amendments are known as the Bill of Rights and, because of their adoption so closely following the adoption of the Constitution itself, are generally considered almost a part of the original document. The first eight of these amendments deal with specific individual rights. The last two are more general in application. The Bill of Rights as a whole guarantees such substantive rights as freedom of speech, of religion and of the press, and such procedural rights as trial by jury and speedy and public trials.

AMENDMENT XI. The amendment was proposed as a result

of the case of *Chisholm* vs. *Georgia* in which a citizen of South Carolina secured a judgment against Georgia. It provides that a state can no longer be compelled to defend itself in the federal courts against a citizen of another state.

AMENDMENT XII. In the election of 1800 Jefferson and Burr received the same number of electoral votes for President because of the provision in Article II that each elector should cast two votes without indicating which was for President and which for Vice-President. To prevent a repetition the manner of casting electoral votes was changed so that each elector shall cast one vote for President and one for Vice-President.

AMENDMENT XIII. This, the first of the Civil War amendments, abolished slavery. It was declared ratified in 1865.

AMENDMENT XIV. This, the second of the Civil War amendments, has been the source of much litigation and interpretation. Section 1 constitutionally defines citizenship for the first time and adds that "No State shall make or enforce any law which shall abridge the privilege or immunities of citizens of the United States; nor shall any State deprive any person of life, liberty, or property, without due process of law; nor deny to any person within its jurisdiction the equal protection of the laws." Section 2 was a threat to the South in that it was an attempt to force enfranchisement of the Negroes on these states under penalty of having membership in the House of Representatives curtailed in proportion to the number of citizens not allowed to vote. Section 3 permitted Congress to remove the disabilities incurred by Southerners for participation in the Confederacy. Section 4 made invalid any debts incurred in support of the rebellion against the United States or claims for the loss of slaves.

AMENDMENT XV. The third and last Civil War amendment prohibits the denial of the suffrage on account of race, color, or previous condition of servitude.

AMENDMENT XVI. Article I, Section 9, clause 4 of the Constitution provides that "No capitation or other direct tax shall be laid, unless in proportion to the census or enumeration hereintofore directed to be taken". Under this provision the Supreme Court had declared an income tax invalid. This amendment authorizes Congress to levy such a tax.

AMENDMENT XVII. Article I called for the election of Senators by the legislatures of the states. This amendment substituted direct popular vote.

AMENDMENT XVIII. Probably the most controversial amendment to the Constitution. It prohibited the manufacture and sale of intoxicating liquors. It was ratified in 1920 and repealed in 1933. It thus became the first amendment to the Constitution to be subsequently repealed.

AMENDMENT XIX. Gave suffrage to women.

AMENDMENT XX. This amendment changed the annual sessions of Congress from the first Monday in December to January 3, thus destroying the "Lame Duck" session of Congress, which, under the old date for the assembly of Congress, brought back to that body for another session those who had been defeated at the polls. It also shortened the second term of President Roosevelt by the difference between March 4, the old date for the inauguration, and January 20, the new date.

AMENDMENT XXI. Repeal of the XVIII Amendment.

AMENDMENT XXII. Limits President to two elective terms.

AMENDMENT XXIII. Gives three electoral votes to the District of Columbia.

AMENDMENT XXIV. Prohibits the use of a poll tax in federal elections.

AMENDMENT XXV. Provides line of succession in case of disability of the President.

AMENDMENT XXVI. Prohibits either the United States or a State from abridging the right of citizens who are 18 years of age to vote because of age.

The Constitution of the United States

We, the people of the United States, in order to form a more perfect union, establish justice, insure domestic tranquility, provide for the common defense, promote the general welfare, and secure the blessings of liberty to ourselves and our posterity, do ordain and establish this Constitution for the United States of America.

ARTICLE I

SECTION I

All legislative powers herein granted shall be vested in a Congress of the United States, which shall consist of a Senate and House of Representatives.

SECTION II

The House of Representatives shall be composed of members chosen every second year by the people of the several States, and the electors in each State shall have the qualifications requisite for electors of the most numerous branch of the State legislature.

No person shall be a Representative who shall not have attained to the age of twenty-five years, and been seven years a citizen of the United States, and who shall not, when elected, be an inhabitant of that State in which he shall be chosen.

Representatives and direct taxes shall be apportioned among the several States which may be included within this Union, according to their respective numbers, *which shall be determined by adding to the whole number of free persons, including those bound to service for a term of years,*[1] and excluding Indians not taxed, *three-fifths of all other persons.*[2] The actual enumeration shall be made within three years after the first meeting of the Congress of the United States, and within every subsequent term of ten years, in such manner as they shall by law direct. The number of Representatives shall not exceed one for every thirty thousand, but each State shall have at last one Representative; *and until such enumeration shall be made, the State of New Hampshire shall be entitled to choose three, Massachusetts eight,*

---

1. Altered by the Fourteenth Amendment.
2. Rescinded by the Fourteenth Amendment.

Rhode Island and Providence Plantations one, Connecticut five, New York six, New Jersey four, Pennsylvania eight, Deleware one, Maryland six, Virginia ten, North Carolina five, South Carolina five, and Georgia three.[3]

When vacancies happen in the representation from any State, the executive authority thereof shall issue writs of election to fill such vacancies.

The House of Representatives shall choose their Speaker and other officers, and shall have the sole power of impeachment.

SECTION III

The Senate of the United States shall be composed of two Senators from each State, *chosen by the legislature thereof,*[4] for six years; and each Senator shall have one vote.

Immediately after they shall be assembled in consequence of the first election, they shall be divided as equally as may be into three classes. The seats of the Senators of the first class shall be vacated at the expiration of the second year, of the second class at the expiration of the fourth year, and of the third class at the expiration of the sixth year, so that one third may be chosen every second year; *and if vacancies happen by resignation or otherwise during the recess of the legislature of any State the executive thereof may make temporary appointments until the next meeting of the legislature, which shall then fill such vacancies.*[5]

No person shall be a Senator who shall not have attained to the age of thirty years, and been nine years a citizen of the United States, and who shall not, when elected, be an inhabitant of that State for which he shall be chosen.

The Vice-President of the United States shall be President of the Senate, but shall have no vote, unless they be equally divided.

The Senate shall choose their other officers, and also a President *pro tempore* in the absence of the Vice-President or when he shall exercise the office of the President of the United States.

The Senate shall have the sole power to try all impeachments. When sitting for that purpose, they shall be on oath or affirmation. When the President of the United States is tried, the Chief Justice shall preside; and no person shall be convicted without the concurrence of two thirds of the members present.

Judgment in cases of impeachment shall not extend further than to removal from office, and disqualification to hold and en-

---

3. Temporary provision.
4. Modified by the Seventeenth Amendment.
5. Modified by the Seventeenth Amendment.

joy any office of honor, trust, or profit under the United States; but the party convicted shall, nevertheless, be liable and subject to indictment, trial, judgment, and punishment, according to law.

SECTION IV

The times, places, and manner of holding elections for Senators and Representatives shall be prescribed in each State by the legislature thereof; but the Congress may at any time by law make or alter such regulations, except as to the places of choosing Senators.

The Congress shall assemble at least once in every year, and such meeting shall be on the first Monday in December, unless they shall by law appoint a different day.[6]

SECTION V

Each house shall be the judge of the elections, returns, and qualifications of its own members, and a majority of each shall constitute a quorum to do business; but a smaller number may adjourn from day to day, and may be authorized to compel the attendance of absent members, in such manner, and under such penalties, as each house may provide.

Each house may determine the rules of its proceedings, punish its members for disorderly behavior, and with the concurrence of two thirds, expel a member.

Each house shall keep a journal of its proceedings, and from time to time publish the same, excepting such parts as may in their judgment require secrecy, and the yeas and nays of the members of either house on any question shall, at the desire of one fifth of those present, be entered on the journal.

Neither house, during the session of Congress, shall, without the consent of the other, adjourn for more than three days, nor to any other place than that in which the two houses shall be sitting.

SECTION VI

The Senators and Representatives shall receive a compensation for their services, to be ascertained by law and paid out of the Treasury of the United States. They shall, in all cases except treason, felony, and breach of the peace, be privileged from arrest during their attendance at the sesson of their respective houses, and in going to and returning from the same; and for any speech or debate in either house they shall not be questioned in any other place.

No Senator or Representative shall, during the time for which

6. Superseded by the Twentieth Amendment.

he was elected, be appointed to any civil office under the authority of the United States, which shall have been created, or the emoluments whereof shall have been increased, during such time; and no person holding any office under the United States shall be a member of either house during his continuance in office.

SECTION VII

All bills for raising revenue shall originate in the House of Representatives; but the Senate may propose or concur with amendments as on other bills.

Every bill which shall have passed the House of Representatives and the Senate shall, before it become a law, be presented to to the President of the United States; if he approves he shall sign it, but if not he shall return it, with his objections, to that house in which it shall have originated, who shall enter the objections at large on their journal and proceed to reconsider it. If after such reconsideration two thirds of that house shall agree to pass the bill, it shall be sent, together with the objections, to the other house, by which it shall likewise be reconsidered, and if approved by two thirds of that house it shall become a law. But in all such cases the votes of both houses shall be determined by yeas and nays, and the names of the persons voting for and against the bill shall be entered on the journal of each house respectively. If any bill shall not be returned by the President within ten days (Sundays excepted) after it shall have been presented to him, the same shall be a law, in like manner as if he had signed it, unless the Congress by their adjournment prevent its return, in which case it shall not be a law.

Every order, resolution, or vote to which the concurrence of the Senate and House of Representatives may be necessary (except on a question of adjournment) shall be presented to the President of the United States; and before the same shall take effect, shall be approved by him, or being disapproved by him, shall be repassed by two thirds of the Senate and House of Representatives, according to the rules and limitations prescribed in the case of a bill.

SECTION VIII

The Congress shall have power to lay and collect taxes, duties, imposts, and excises, to pay the debts and provide for the common defense and general welfare of the United States; but all duties, imposts, and excises shall be uniform throughout the United States.

To borrow money on the credit of the United States.

To regulate commerce with foreign nations and among the several States, and with the Indian tribes;

To establish a uniform rule of naturalization, and uniform laws on the subject of bankruptcies throughout the United States;

To coin money, regulate the value thereof, and of foreign coin, and fix the standard of weights and measures;

To provide for the punishment of counterfeiting the securities and current coin of the United States;

To establish post-offices and post-roads;

To promote the progress of science and useful arts by securing for limited times to authors and inventors the exclusive rights to their respective writings and discoveries.

To constitute tribunals inferior to the Supreme Court;

To define and punish piracies and felonies committed on the high seas and offenses against the law of nations;

To declare war, grant letters of marque and reprisal, and make rules concerning captures on land and water;

To raise and support armies, but no appropriation of money to that use shall be for a longer term than two years;

To provide and maintain a navy;

To make rules for the government and regulation of the land and naval forces.

To provide for calling forth the militia to execute the laws of the Union, suppress insurrections, and repel invasions;

To provide for organizing, arming, and disciplining the militia, and for governing such part of them as may be employed in the service of the United States, reserving to the States respectively the appointment of the officers, and the authority of training the militia according to the discipline prescribed by Congress;

To exercise exclusive legislation in all cases whatsoever over such district (not exceeding ten miles square) as may, by cession of particular States and the acceptance of Congress, become the seat of the Government of the United States, and to exercise like authority over all places purchased by the consent of the legislature of the State in which the same shall be, for the erection of forts, magazines, arsenals, dockyards, and other needful buildings; and

To make all laws which shall be necessary and proper for carrying into execution the foregoing powers, and all other powers vested by this Constitution in the Government of the United States, or in any department or officer thereof.

SECTION IX

The migration or importation of such persons as any of the States now existing shall think proper to admit shall not be pro-

hibited by the Congress prior to the year one thousand eight hundred and eight, but a tax or duty may be imposed on such importation, not exceeding ten dollars for each person.[7]

The privilege of the writ of *habeas corpus* shall not be suspended, unless when in case of rebellion or invasion the public safety may require it.

No bill of attainder or *ex post facto* law shall be passed.

No capitation or other direct tax shall be laid, unless in proportion to the census or enumeration hereinbefore directed to be taken.

No tax or duty shall be laid on articles exported from any State.

No preference shall be given by any regulation of commerce or revenue to the ports of one State over those of another; nor shall vessels bound to or from one State be obliged to enter, clear, or pay duties in another.

No money shall be drawn from the Treasury but in consequence of appropriations made by law; and a regular statement and account of the receipts and expenditures of all public money shall be published from time to time.

No title of nobility shall be granted by the United States; and no person holding any office of profit or trust under them shall, without the consent of the Congress, accept of any present, emolument, office, or title, of any kind whatever, from any king, prince, or foreign State.

SECTION X

No State shall enter into any treaty, alliance, or confederation; grant letters of marque and reprisal; coin money; emit bills of credit; make anything but gold and silver coin a tender in payment of debts; pass any bill of attainder, *ex post facto* law, or law impairing the obligation of contracts, or grant any title of nobility.

No State shall, without the consent of Congress, lay any imposts or duties on imports or exports, except what may be absolutely necessary for executing its inspection laws; and the net produce of all duties and imposts, laid by any State on imports or exports, shall be for the use of the Treasury of the United States; and all such laws shall be subject to the revision and control of the Congress.

No State shall, without the consent of Congress, lay any duty of tonnage, keep troops or ships of war in time of peace, enter

7. Temporary provision.

into any agreement or compact with another State or with a foreign power, or engage in war, unless actually invaded or in such imminent danger as will not admit of delay.

ARTICLE II

SECTION I

The executive power shall be vested in a President of the United States of America. He shall hold his office during the term of four years, and together with the Vice-President, chosen for the same term, be elected as follows:

Each State shall appoint, in such manner as the legislature thereof may direct, a number of electors, equal to the whole number of Senators and Representatives to which the State may be entitled in the Congress; but no Senator or Representative, or person holding an office of trust or profit under the United States, shall be appointed an elector.

The electors shall meet in their respective States and vote by ballot for two persons, of whom one at least shall not be an inhabitant of the same State with themselves. And they shall make a list of all the persons voted for, and of the number of votes for each; which list they shall sign and certify, and transmit sealed to the seat of government of the United States, directed to the President of the Senate. The President of the Senate shall, in the presence of the Senate and House of Representatives, open all the certificates, and the votes shall then be counted. The person having the greatest number of votes shall be the President, if such number be a majority of the whole number of electors appointed; and if there be more than one who have such a majority, and have an equal number of votes, then the House of Representatives shall immediately choose by ballot one of them for President; and if no person have a majority, then from the five highest on the list the said House shall in like manner choose the President. But in choosing the President the votes shall be taken by States, the representation from each State having one vote; a quorum for this purpose shall consist of a member or members from two thirds of the States, and a majority of all the States shall be necessary to a choice. In every case, after the choice of the President, the person having the greatest number of votes of the electors shall be the Vice-President. But if there should remain two or more who have equal votes, the Senate shall choose from them by ballot the Vice-President[8]

8. Superseded by the Twelfth Amendment.

The Congress may determine the time of choosing the electors and the day on which they shall give their votes, which day shall be the same throughout the United States.

No person except a natural-born citizen, or a citizen of the United States at the time of the adoption of this Constitution, shall be eligible to the office of President; neither shall any person be eligible to that office who shall not have attained to the age of thirty-five years, and been fourteen years a resident within the United States.

In case of the removal of the President from office, or of his death, resignation, or inability to discharge the powers and duties of the said office, the same shall devolve on the Vice-President, and the Congress may by law provide for the case of removal, death, resignation, or inability, both of the President and Vice-President, declaring what officer shall then act as President, and such officer shall act accordingly until the disability be removed or a President shall be elected.

The President shall, at stated times, receive for his services a compensation which shall neither be increased nor diminished during the period for which he may have been elected, and he shall not receive within that period any other emolument from the United States or any of them.

Before he enter on the execution of his office he shall take the following oath or affirmation:

"I do solemnly swear (or affirm) that I will faithfully execute the office of President of the United States, and will to the best of my ability preserve, protect, and defend the Constitution of the United States."

SECTION II

The President shall be commander-in-chief of the army and navy of the United States, and of the militia of the several States when called into the actual service of the United States; he may require the opinion, in writing, of the principal officer in each of the executive departments, upon any subject relating to the duties of their respective offices, and he shall have power to grant reprieves and pardons for offenses against the United States, except in cases of impeachment.

He shall have power, by and with the advice and consent of the Senate, to make treaties, provided two thirds of the Senators present concur; and he shall nominate, and, by and with the advice and consent of the Senate, shall appoint ambassadors, other public ministers and consuls, judges of the Supreme Court, and all other officers of the United States, whose appointments are not herein otherwise provided for, and which shall be established by law; but the Congress may by law vest the appointment of such inferior officers, as they think proper, in the President alone, in the courts of law, or in the heads of departments.

The President shall have power to fill up all vacancies that may happen during the recess of the Senate, by granting commissions which shall expire at the end of their next session.

SECTION III

He shall from time to time give to the Congress information of the state of the Union, and recommend to their consideration such measures as he shall judge necessary and expedient; he may, on extraordinary occasions, convene both houses, or either of them, and in case of disagreement between them with respect to the time of adjournment, he may adjourn them to such time as he shall think proper; he shall receive ambassadors and other public ministers; he shall take care that the laws be faithfully executed, and shall commission all the officers of the United States.

SECTION IV

The President, Vice-President, and all civil officers of the United States shall be removed from office on impeachment for and conviction of treason, bribery, or other high crimes and misdemeanors.

ARTICLE III

SECTION I

The judicial power of the United States shall be vested in one Supreme Court, and in such inferior courts as the Congress may from time to time ordain and establish. The judges, both of the supreme and inferior courts, shall hold their offices during good behavior, and shall, at stated times, receive for their services a compensation which shall not be diminished during their continuance in office.

SECTION II

The judicial power shall extend to all cases, in law and equity, arising under this Constitution, the laws of the United States, and the treaties made, or which shall be made, under their authority; to all cases affecting ambassadors, other public ministers, and consuls; to all cases of admiralty and maritime jurisdiction; to controversies to which the United States shall be a party; to controversies between two or more States; *between a State and citizens of another State;*[9] between citizens of different States; be-

9. Restricted by the Eleventh Amendment.

tween citizens of the same State claiming lands under grants of different States, and between a State, or the citizens thereof, and foreign States, citizens, or subjects.

In all cases affecting ambassadors, other public ministers, and consuls, and those in which a State shall be a party, the Supreme Court shall have original jurisdiction. In all the other cases before mentioned the Supreme Court shall have appellate jurisdiction, both as to law and fact, with such exceptions and under such regulations as the Congress shall make.

The trial of all crimes, except in cases of impeachment, shall be by jury; and such trial shall be held in the State where the said crimes shall have been committed, but when not committed within any State, the trial shall be at such place or places as the Congress may by law have directed.

SECTION III

Treason against the United States shall consist only in levying war against them, or in adhering to their enemies, giving them aid and comfort. No person shall be convicted of treason unless on the testimony of two witnesses to the same overt act, or on confession in open court.

The Congress shall have power to declare the punishment of treason, but no attainder of treason shall work corruption of blood or forfeiture except during the life of the person attainted.

ARTICLE IV

SECTION I

Full faith and credit shall be given in each State to the public acts, records, and judicial proceedings of every other State. And the Congress may by general laws prescribe the manner in which such acts, records, and proceedings shall be proved, and the effect thereof.

SECTION II

The citizens of each State shall be entitled to all privileges and immunities of citizens in the several States.[10]

A person charged in any State with treason, felony, or other crime, who shall flee from justice, and be found in another State, shall, on demand of the executive authority of the State from which he fled, be delivered up, to be removed to the State having jurisdiction of the crime.

---

10. Extended by the Fourteenth Amendment.

No person held to service or labor in one State, under the laws thereof, escaping into another, shall, in consequence of any law or regulation therein, be discharged from such service or labor, but shall be delivered up on claim of the party to whom such service or labor may be due.[11]

SECTION III

New States may be admitted by the Congress into this Union; but no new State shall be formed or erected within the jurisdiction of any other State; nor any State be formed by the junction of two more States or parts of States, without the consent of the legislatures of the States concerned as well as of the Congress.

The Congress shall have power to dispose of and make all needful rules and regulations respecting the territory or other property belonging to the United States; and nothing in this Constitution shall be so construed as to prejudice any claims of the United States or any particular State.

SECTION IV

The United States shall guarantee to every State in this Union a republican form of government, and shall protect each of them against invasion, and on application of the legislature, or of the executive (when the legislature cannot be convened), against domestic violence.

ARTICLE V

The Congress, whenever two thirds of both houses shall deem it necessary, shall propose amendments to this Constitution, or, on the application of the legislatures of two thirds of the several States, shall call a convention for proposing amendments, which in either case shall be valid to all intents and purposes as part of this Constitution, when ratified by the legislatures of three fourths of the several States, or by conventions in three fourths thereof, as the one or the other mode of ratification may be proposed by the Congress, *provided that no amendments which may be made prior to the year one thousand eight hundred and eight shall in any manner affect the first and fourth clauses in the ninth section of the first article,*[12] and that no State, without its consent, shall be deprived of its equal suffrage in the Senate.

---

11. Superseded by the Thirteenth Amendment in so far as pertaining to slaves.

12. Temporary clause.

ARTICLE VI

All debt contracted and engagements entered into, before the adoption of this Constitution, shall be as valid against the United States under this Constitution as under the confederation.[13]

This Constitution, and the laws of the United States, which shall be made in pursuance thereof, and all treaties made, or which shall be made, under the authority of the United States, shall be the supreme law of the land; and the judges in every State shall be bound thereby, anything in the Constitution or laws of any State to the contrary notwithstanding.

The Senators and Representatives before mentioned, and the members of the several State legislatures, and all executive and judicial officers both of the United States and of the several States, shall be bound by oath or affirmation to support this Constitution; but no religious test shall ever be required as a qualification to any office or public trust under the United States.

ARTICLE VII

The ratification of the conventions of nine States shall be sufficient for the establishment of this Constitution between the States so ratifying the same.

Done in convention by the unanimous consent of the States present, the seventeenth day of September, in the year of our Lord one thousand seven hundred and eighty-seven, and of the independence of the United States of America the twelfth. In witness whereof, we have hereunto subscribed our names.

[Signed by][14]

AMENDMENTS

I. Congress shall make no law respecting an establishment of religion, or prohibiting the free exercise thereof; or abridging the freedom of speech or of the press; or the right of the people peaceably to assemble, and to petition the government for a redress of grievances.

II. A well-regulated militia being necessary to the security of a free state, the right of the people to keep and bear arms shall not be infringed.

III. No soldier shall, in time of peace, be quartered in any

---

13. Extended by the Fourteenth Amendment.
14. The signatures are omitted here.

house without the consent of the owner, nor in time of war, but in a manner to be prescribed by law.

IV. The right of the people to be secure in their persons, houses, papers, and effects, against unreasonable searches and seizures, shall not be violated, and no warrants shall issue but upon probable cause, supported by oath or affirmation, and particularly describing the place to be searched, and the person or things to be seized.

V. No person shall be held to answer for a capital or otherwise infamous crime, unless on a presentment or indictment of a grand jury, except in cases arising in the land or naval forces, or in the militia, when in actual service in time of war or public danger; nor shall any person be subject for the same offense to be twice put in jeopardy of life or limb; nor shall be compelled in any criminal case to be a witness against himself, nor be deprived of life, liberty, or property, without due process of law; nor shall private property be taken for public use without just compensation.

VI. In all criminal prosecutions the accused shall enjoy the right to a speedy and public trial, by an impartial jury of the State and district wherein the crime shall have been committed, which district shall have been previously ascertained by law, and to be informed of the nature and cause of the accusation; to be confronted with the witnesses against him; to have compulsory process for obtaining witnesses in his favor, and to have the assistance of counsel for his defense.

VII. In suits at common law, where the value in controversy shall exceed twenty dollars, the right of trial by jury shall be preserved, and no fact tried by a jury shall be otherwise re-examined in any court of the United States, than according to the rules of the common law.

VIII. Excessive bail shall not be required, nor excessive fines imposed, nor cruel and unusual punishments inflicted.

IX. The enumeration in the Constitution of certain rights shall not be construed to deny or disparage others retained by the people.

X[15] The powers not delegated to the United States by the Constitution, nor prohibited by it to the States, are reserved to the States respectively, or to the people.

XI[16] The judicial power of the United States shall not be construed to extend to any suit in law or equity, commenced or

15. The first ten amendments took effect December 15, 1791.
16. Proclaimed January 8, 1798.

prosecuted against one of the United States by citizens of another State, or by citizens or subjects of any foreign State.

XII.[17] The electors shall meet in their respective States and vote by ballot for President and Vice-President, one of whom, at least, shall not be an inhabitant of the same State with themselves; they shall name in their ballots the person voted for as President, and in distinct ballots the person voted for as Vice-President, and they shall make distinct lists of all persons voted for as President and of all persons voted for as Vice-President, and of the number of votes for each; which lists they shall sign and certify, and transmit sealed to the seat of the government of the United States, directed to the President of the Senate. The President of the Senate shall, in the presence of the Senate and House of Representatives, open all the certificates and the votes shall then be counted. The person having the greatest number of votes for President shall be the President, if such number be a majority of the whole number of electors appointed; and if no person have such a majority, then from the person having the highest numbers not exceeding three on the list of those voted for as President, the House of Representatives shall choose immediately, by ballot, the President. But in choosing the President the votes shall be taken by States, the representation from each State having one vote; a quorum for this purpose shall consist of a member or members from two thirds of the States, and a majority of all States shall be necessary to a choice. And if the House of Representatives shall not choose a President whenever the right of choice shall devolve upon them, before the *fourth day of March*[18] next following, then the Vice-President shall act as President, as in the case of the death or other constitutional disability of the President.

The person having the greatest number of votes as Vice-President shall be the Vice-President, if such number be a majority of the whole number of electors appointed; and if no person have a majority, then from the two highest numbers on the list the Senate shall choose the Vice-President: a quorum for the purpose shall consist of two thirds of the whole number of Senators, and a majority of the whole number shall be necessary to a choice. But no person constitutionally ineligible to the office of President shall be eligible to that of Vice-President of the United States.

---

17. Proclaimed September 25, 1804.
18. Superseded by the Twentieth Amendment.

XIII.[19] *Section* 1. Neither slavery nor involuntary servitude, except as a punishment for crime whereof the party shall have been duly convicted, shall exist within the United States or any place subject to their jurisdiction.

XIV.[20] *Section* 1. All persons born or naturalized in the United States, and subject to the jurisdiction thereof, are citizens of the United States and of the State wherein they reside. No State shall make or enforce any law which shall abridge the privileges or immunities of citizens of the United States; nor shall any State deprive any person of life, liberty, or property, without due process of law; nor deny to any person within its jurisdiction the equal protection of the laws.

Section 2. Representatives shall be apportioned among the several States according to their respective numbers, counting the whole number of persons in each State, excluding Indians not taxed. But when the right to vote at any election for the choice of electors for President and Vice-President of the United States, Representatives in Congress, the executive and judicial officers of a State, or the members of the legislature thereof, is denied to any of the male inhabitants of such State, being twenty-one years of age, and citizens of the United States, or in any way abridged, except for participation in rebellion, or other crime, the basis of representation therein shall be reduced in the proportion which the number of such male citizens shall bear to the whole number of male citizens twenty-one years of age in such State.

Section 3. No person shall be a Senator or Representative in Congress, or elector of President and Vice-President, or hold any office, civil or military, under the United States or under any State, who, having previously taken an oath as a member of Congress, or as an officer of the United States, or as a member of any State legislature, or as an executive or judicial officer of any State, to support the Constitution of the United States, shall have engaged in insurrection or rebellion against the same, or given aid or comfort to the enemies thereof. But Congress may, by a vote of two thirds of each house, remove such disability

Section 4. The validity of the public debt of the United States, authorized by law, including debts incurred for payment of pensions and bounties for services in suppressing insurrection or re-

19. Proclaimed December 18, 1865.
20. Proclaimed July 28, 1868.

bellion, shall not be questioned. But neither the United States nor any State shall assume or pay any debt or obligation incurred in aid of insurrection or rebellion against the United States, or any claim for the loss or emancipation of any slave; but all such debts, obligations, and claims shall be held illegal and void.

Section 5. The Congress shall have power to enforce, by appropriate legislation, the provisions of this article.

XV[21] *Section* 1. The right of citizens of the United States to vote shall not be denied or abridged by the United States or by any State on account of race, color, or previous condition of servitude.

Section 2. The Congress shall have power to enforce this article by appropriate legislation.

XVI.[22] The Congress shall have power to lay and collect taxes on incomes, from whatever source derived, without apportionment among the several States, and without regard to any census or enumeration.

XVII[23] The Senate of the United States shall be composed of two Senators from each State, elected by the people thereof, for six years; and each Senator shall have one vote. The electors in each State shall have the qualifications requisite for electors of the most numerous branch of the State legislature.

When vacancies happen in the representation of any State in the Senate, the executive authority of such State shall issue writs of election to fill such vacancies: *Provided*, That the legislature of any State may empower the executive thereof to make temporary appointments until the people fill the vacancies by election as the legislature may direct.

This amendment shall not be so construed as to affect the election or term of any Senator chosen before it becomes valid as part of the Constitution.

XVIII[24] SECTION 1. *After one year from the ratification of this article the manufacture, sale, or transportation of intoxicating liquors within, the importation thereof into, or the exportation thereof from the United States and all territory subject to the jurisdiction thereof for beverage purposes is hereby prohibited.*

SECTION 2. *The Congress and the several States shall have concurrent power to enforce this article by appropriate legislation.*

---

21. Proclaimed March 30, 1870
22. Proclaimed February 25, 1913
23. Proclaimed May 31, 1913.
24. Proclaimed January 29, 1919.

SECTION 3. *This article shall be inoperative unless it shall have ratified as an amendment to the Constitution by the legislatures of the several States, as provided in the Constitution, within seven years from the date of the submission hereof to the States by the Congress.*[25]

XIX.[26] *Section* 1. The right of citizens of the United States to vote shall not be denied or abridged by the United States or by any State on account of sex.

Section 2. Congress shall have power to enforce this article by appropriate legislation.

XX.[27] *Section* 1. The terms of the President and Vice-President shall end at noon on the 20th day of January, and the terms of Senators and Representatives at noon on the 3rd day of January, of the years in which such terms would have ended if this article had not been ratified; and the terms of their successors shall then begin.

Section 2. The Congress shall assemble at least once in every year, and such meeting shall begin at noon on the 3rd day of January, unless they shall by law appoint a different day.

Section 3. If at the time fixed for the beginning of the term of the President, the President-elect shall have died, the Vice-President-elect shall become President. If a President shall not have been chosen before the time fixed for the beginning of his term, or if the President-elect shall have failed to qualify, then the Vice-President-elect shall act as President until a President shall have qualified, and the Congress may by law provide for the case wherein neither a President-elect nor a Vice-President-elect shall have qualified, declaring who shall then act as President, or the manner in which one who is to act shall be selected, and such person shall act accordingly until a President or Vice-President shall have qualified.

Section 4. The Congress may by law provide for the case of the death of any of the persons from whom the House of Representatives may choose a President whenever the right of choice shall have devolved upon them, and for the case of the death of any of the persons from whom the Senate may choose a Vice-President whenever the right of choice shall have devolved upon them.

---

25. Rescinded by the Twenty-first Amendment.
26. Proclaimed August 26, 1920.
27. Proclaimed February 6, 1933.

Section 5. Sections 1 and 2 shall take effect on the 15th day of October following the ratification of this article.

Section 6. This article shall be inoperative unless it shall have been ratified as an amendment to the Constitution by the legislatures of three-fourths of the several States within seven years from the date of its submission .

XXI.[28] *Section* 1. The Eighteenth article of amendment to the Constitution of the United States is hereby repealed.

Section 2. The transportation or importation into any State, territory, or possession of the United States for delivery or use therein of intoxicating liquors, in violation of the laws thereof, is hereby prohibited.

Section 3. This article shall be inoperative unless it shall have been ratified as an amendment to the Constitution by conventions in the several States, as provided in the Constitution, within seven years from the date of the submission hereof to the States by the Congress.

XXII.[29] *Section* 1. No person shall be elected to the office of the President more than twice, and no person who has held the office of President, or acted as President, for more than two years of a term to which some other person was elected President shall be elected to the office of President more than once. But this Article shall not apply to any person holding the office of President when this Article was proposed by the Congress, and shall not prevent any person who may be holding the office of President, or acting as President, during the term within which this Article becomes operative from holding the office of President or acting as President during the remainder of such term.

XXIII.[30] *Section* 1. The District constituting the seat of Government of the United States shall appoint in such manner as the Congress may direct:

A number of electors of President and Vice President equal to the whole number of Senators and Representatives in Congress to which the District would be entitled if it were a State, but in no event more than the least populous State; they shall be in addition to those appointed by the States, but they shall be considered, for the purposes of the election of President and Vice President, to be electors appointed by a State; and they

---

28. Proclaimed December 5, 1933.
29. Proclaimed March 3, 1951.
30. Ratified May 29, 1961.

shall meet in the District and perform such duties as provided by the twelfth article of amendment.

Section 2. The Congress shall have power to enforce this article by appropriate legislation.

XXIV.[31] *Section* 1. The right of citizens of the United States to vote in any primary or other election for President or Vice-President, or for Senators or Representatives in Congress, shall not be denied or abridged by the United States or any State by reason of failure to pay any poll tax or other tax.

Section 2. The Congress shall have power to enforce this article by appropriate legislation.

XXV.[32] *Section* 1. In case of the removal of the President from office or of his death or resignation, the Vice President shall become President.

Section 2. Whenever there is a vacancy in the office of the Vice President, the President shall nominate a Vice President who shall take office upon confirmation by a majority vote of both Houses of Congress.

Section 3. Whenever the President transmits to the President pro tempore of the Senate and the Speaker of the House of Representatives his written declaration that he is unable to discharge the powers and duties of his office, and until he transmits to them a written declaration to the contrary, such powers and duties shall be discharged by the Vice President as Acting President.

Section 4 Whenever the Vice President and a majority of either the principal officers of the executive departments or of such other body as Congress may by law provide, transmit to the President pro tempore of the Senate and the Speaker of the House of Representatives their written declaration that the President is unable to discharge the powers and duties of his office, the Vice President shall immediately assume the powers and duties of the office as Acting President.

Thereafter, when the President transmit to the President pro tempore of the Senate and the Speaker of the House of Representatives his written declaration that no inability exists, he shall resume the powers and duties of his office unless the Vice President and a majority of either the principal officers of the executive departments or of such other body as Congress may by law provide, transmit within four days to the President pro tempore of the Senate and the Speaker of the House of Repre-

31. Certified February 5, 1964.
32. Certified February 23, 1967.

sentatives their written declaration that the President is unable to discharge the powers and duties of his office. Thereupon Congress shall decide the issue, assembling within forty-eight hours for that purpose if not in session. If the Congress, within twenty-one days after receipt of the latter written declaration, or, if Congress is not in session, within twenty-one days after Congress is required to assemble, determines by a two-thirds vote of both Houses that the President is unable to discharge the powers and duties of his office, the Vice President shall continue to discharge the same as Acting President; otherwise, the President shall resume the powers and duties of his office.

XXVI. Section 1. The right of citizens of the United States, who are 18 years of age or older, to vote shall not be denied or abridged by the United States or by any State on account of age.

Section 2. The Congress shall have power to enforce this article by appropriate legislation.[33]

33. Certified July 7, 1971.

Questions on the Constitution of the United States

PART I

History and Fundamental Principles

1. Explain fully the meaning of "constitutional government."
2. What was the first national government of the United States? What powers did it exercise? How long did it last?
3. What was the first written constitution of the United States? Just when and how long was it in effect? Was it satisfactory? What were its defects?
4. When and where was the Federal Convention held? How many delegates attended? How many signed the Constitution? Was Thomas Jefferson present? Who were the most prominent delegates? What class of people did the delegates represent?
5. Describe the organization and procedure of the Federal Convention. What were the two great plans of union? Give the provisions of each?
6. Explain why the Constitution is often referred to as "a bundle of compromises." Give the provision of the principal compromises.
7. What are the provisions of Article VII? What objections were raised against the Constitution? When did it go into effect? Had all of the states ratified at this time?
8. How does a federal government differ from a unitary government? Explain the terms "delegated," "implied," "reserved," "inherent," and "enumerated" powers.
9. Explain what is meant by "the separation of powers," and "checks and balances."
10. Give an example of judicial review and explain fully the fundamental principles of government involved.

PART II

The Constitution as an Objective Document

I. *General.*

1. Compare the length of the Constitution of the United States to that of Georgia.

2. Describe the arrangement of the Constitution. How many articles are there?
3. Describe the wording. Are there any repetitions? Criticise the use of broad terms.

II. *Preamble.*

1. What is the meaning of the opening words, "We, the People of the United States. . . ."?
2. What were the objects of establishing the Constitution?

III. *Article I.*

1. With what subject does Article I deal? Is there any significance to this arrangement?
2. How many members are there in the House of Representatives? How is this number determined? How apportioned?
3. Who can vote for representatives?
4. How are vacancies in the House filled?
5. What are the qualifications of representatives?
6. Who presides over the House? How is he chosen? What power does he exercise?
7. How can you explain the equal representation of the States in the Senate?
8. What was the original method of choosing senators?
9. What is meant by describing the Senate as a continuous body? What is the term of a Senator?
10. What are the qualifications for a Senator?
11. Who presides over the Senate? How is he chosen? Compare his powers to those of the Speaker of the House.
12. Describe the process of impeachment.
13. What action has Congress taken under Article I, Section 4, Clause I, in regard to the time, places, and manner of holding elections?
14. What is the term of "a Congress"? How often does it have to meet? May it meet oftener? How did Amendment XX affect the time of meeting? Do we still have "long" and "short" sessions?
15. Give the powers and duties of each house, and the privileges of members prescribed in Sections 5 and 6.
16. Would the adoption of the cabinet system of government necessitate an amending of the Constitution?
17. What provision is made in regard to revenue measures? How is the spirit of this violated in practice?

18. Explain how a bill is introduced and passed.
19. Summarize the powers of Congress found in Section 8. Why is the 18th paragraph of this section especially important?
20. What distinct prohibitions are imposed upon the Central Government in Section 9? Can you suggest reasons for these?
21. What distinct prohibitions are imposed upon the State Governments in Section 10?
22. Explain the following terms: "bill of attainder," "writ of habeas corpus," "ex post facto laws," "export taxes."
23. Can a state enter into any treaty? Can a state enter into any "agreement" with another state or a foreign state?
24. How does Article I compare in length with the other articles? How many sections does it contain?

IV. *Article II.*

1. Does the Constitution provide for a plural or single executive? Is there any provision relating to a cabinet? Heads of departments? Is there any distinction between the "cabinet" and the "heads of the executive departments"?
2. What is the term of a president? Can he serve more than two terms?
3. What are the qualifications of the president and vice-president?
4. Describe the original method of electing the president. What changes were made by the 12th Amendment? The 20th?
5. How has the development of political parties affected the method of election? Describe the present method of election.
6. How can a president be removed from office? Discuss the succession to the presidency. How is this determined?
7. What oath is required of the president? Who administers it?
8. Summarize the following powers of the president: (a) military, (b) executive, (c) legislative.
9. What is the address on the "state of the union"?

V. *Article III.*

1. To what extent does the Constitution entrust the organization of the federal judicial system to Congress? What definite provisions are stated to insure a relative independence of the judiciary?

2. Describe the Supreme Court and discuss its importance.
3. Outline the structure of the federal courts as they exist today and summarize the function of each.
4. What is the jurisdiction of the Federal Courts as described by the Constitution?
5. What is meant by "equity"? By "cases of admiralty and maritime jurisdiction"? By "original jurisdiction"? By "appellate jurisdiction"?
6. How is trial by jury safeguarded in the Constitution?
7. How is treason defined? What is meant by "attainder of treason"? By "corruption of blood"?

VI. *Article IV.*

1. What inter-state duties and obligations are specifically laid down in Article IV? Are these of much value?
2. What is the meaning of the "full faith and credit" clause?
3. What is the meaning of the first sentence in Section 2?
4. Describe the process of rendition.
5. Does the word "slave" appear in the body of the Constitution? Are any references made to slave? Does the word appear in the amendments?
6. How may new States be admitted into the Union? Does the territory have to be contiguous?
7. What authority has power over property and land belonging to the U. S.?
8. What is meant by a "republican form of government"? What branch of the national government decides whether a State's government is republican?

VII. *Article V.*

1. In what four ways may the Constitution be amended? How many of these ways have been used?
2. Could the Constitution be so amended as to deprive the smaller states of their "equal suffrage in the Senate"?

VIII. *Article VI.*

1. What is the "supreme law of the land"?
2. In case of a conflict between a State law and a National law, which prevails? Always?
3. What officials are bound by oath to support the Constitution?

IX. *Article VII.*

1. How was the Constitution ratified, by the States or by the people?

X. *Amendments to the Constitution.*

1. Which of the amendments are referred to as the "Bill of Rights"? Why so called? When were they adopted? Summarize the provisions of these amendments.
2. What are some of the rights referred to in the ninth amendment as being retained by the people?
3. Identify the tenth amendment. Was it necessary?
4. Can a State be sued? What led to the eleventh amendment?
5. What led to the twelfth amendment? What are its chief provisions?
6. The thirteenth, fourteenth, and fifteenth amendments were Reconstruction or Civil War amendments. What was each and why was it proposed?
7. Which amendment is longest? Which do you consider most important? Why?
8. Quote section one of the fourteenth amendment and explain the meaning of each of the three clauses in the second sentence. Does the word "person" include corporations? Is the clause ". . . nor shall any State deprive any person of life, liberty or property, without due process of law" a repetition of the statement in the fifth amendment that "No person shall . . . be deprived of life, liberty, or property without due process of law"?
9. Why has section two of the fourteenth amendment never been enforced?
10. Identify the sixteenth amendment and explain the odd wording.
11. In what sense did the seventeenth amendment impair the design of the framers of the Constitution? Was it a wise step?
12. Can one amendment repeal another? What provision does the twenty-first amendment make for the protection of "dry" states?
13. Which three amendments deal with the suffrage? Who can vote for members of Congress? Do we have a uniform electorate?
14. Why is the twentieth amendment called the "lame duck" amendment?
15. On what date will future presidents take office? Members of Congress? How often must Congress meet? Could it change the date of its meetings?

16. What provisions are made for succession to the presidency?
17. What significance is there to the provisions found in the eighteenth, twentieth, and twenty-first amendments limiting the period of ratification to seven years?
18. How did the ratification of the twenty-first amendment differ from the method previously used?
19. Under the twenty-second amendment what are the minimum and maximum limits to Presidential tenure?
20. Do residents of the District of Columbia have any voice in the election of the President?
21. How is a vacancy in the office of Vice President filled?
22. What is the procedure for determining whether the President "is unable to discharge the powers and duties of his office"?

Bibliography

Any good textbook on American government will aid in interpreting the Constitution. Saye, Pound and Allums, *Principles of American Government* (Prentice-Hall, Inc., publishers; frequent revisions) is a text often used at the University. The Department of State has published a *Documentary History of the Constitution of the United States of America, 1786–1870* (3 vols., Washington, 1894–1900). *The Constitution of the United States of America, Analysis and Interpretation* edited by E. S. Corwin (Sen. Doc. 170, 82nd Congress, 2nd Sess.) is a helpful reference. For an extensive and detailed study of the Constitution there can be no substitute for the actual decisions of the Supreme Court. Among the most helpful summaries of these decisions are Gerald Gunther, *Constitutional Law* (Mineola, N.Y.: Foundation Press, 1980), Martin Shapiro and R. T. Tresolini, *American Constitutional Law* (New York: Macmillan Co., 1979), and Albert B. Saye, *American Constitutional Law, Text and Cases* (St. Paul: West Publishing Co., 1979). An excellent short history of the Court is Robert G. McCloskey's *The American Supreme Court* (University of Chicago Press, 1960).

PART II

The Constitution of Georgia

Introduction

"We hold these truths to be self-evident, that all men are created equal, that they are endowed by their Creator with certain unalienable rights, that among these are life, liberty, and the pursuit of Happiness.—That to secure these rights, Governments are instituted among Men, deriving their just powers from the consent of the governed,—That whenever any Form of Government becomes destructive of these ends, it is the Right of the People to alter or to abolish it, and to institute new Government, laying its foundation on such principles and organizing its powers in such form, as to them shall seem most likely to effect their Safety and Happiness." Thus wrote Thomas Jefferson in the American Declaration of Independence.

This doctrine of *popular sovereignty* was emphasized by Abraham Lincoln. In his Gettysburg Address of 1863 he observed that "our fathers brought forth on this continent a new nation, conceived in liberty, and dedicated to the proposition that all men are created equal." He dedicated the nation to the proposition "that government of the people, by the people, for the people shall not perish from the earth." Basically, it was in defense of this proposition that the United States entered World Wars I and II.

While adhering to a doctrine of popular sovereignty, the American people have never advocated unrestrained democracy. They are as deeply attached to the concept of constitutional government—that is to say, *limited government*—as they are to democracy and equality.

CONSTITUTIONAL LAW

"We have learned by heart the Twelve Tables, and we have been accustomed to call other things of this kind laws; but we must remember that all the power these particular laws have to enjoin rightful acts is older than peoples or states, and coeval with God himself, who rules heaven and earth. Reason, springing from the nature of things, which impels us to good and recalls us from evil, did not become law when it was written, but when it was made; and it was made at the same time as the mind of God. Every law which rightly bears the name, is good. Many enactments no more deserve the name of law than if enacted by highwaymen! Law in the highest and true sense is a distinction between things just and unjust, expressing that original and fundamental nature of all things to which the laws of men are conformed which inflict penalties on the wicked and defend and protect the good." Thus wrote the Roman jurist Cicero in *De Legibus* in the first century B.C.

The concept of a higher law has permeated the thought of mankind through the ages. In the United States a noble attempt has been made to insure that true law prevails over injustice through the establishment of constitutional government. We have the Constitution of the United States of America, dating from 1787, and a separate written document as the constitution for each of the fifty states of the Union. These constitutions define the powers of government, divide them between the executive, legislative, and judicial branches, and specify rights of the people that are not to be encroached upon by the government. For example, "Congress shall make no law respecting an establishment of religion, or prohibiting the free exercise thereof." The law stated in a constitution or derived from interpretations thereof (especially interpretations by the courts) is called constitutional law.

Constitutional law is distinguished from statutory law. Theoretically, the constitutional law of a state is confined to basic principles, whereas statutory law deals with less fundamental matters and with details likely to necessitate frequent revision. The inclusion of details such as salaries of officials in state constitutions tends to break down this distinction.

JUDICIAL REVIEW

Americans are familiar with a hierarchy of laws. Article VI of the Constitution of the United States reads: "This Constitution, and the laws of the United States which shall be made in pursuance thereof, and all treaties made, or which shall be made, under the authority of the United States, shall be the supreme law of the land; and the judges in every State shall be bound thereby, anything in the Constitution or laws of any State to the contrary notwithstanding."

In the famous case of *Marbury* vs. *Madison* (1803) the United States Supreme Court declared an act of Congress to be void, thus establishing the practice of judicial review. Chief Justice Marshall wrote: "If an act of the legislature, repugnant to the Constitution, is void, does it, notwithstanding its invalidity, bind the courts, and obligate them to give it effect? Or, in other words, though it be not law, does it constitute a rule as operative as if it was a law? This would be . . . an absurdity too gross to be insisted on."

The principle of judicial review is well established in America.

The Bill of Rights of the Georgia Constitution contains this specific clause: "Legislative acts in violation of this Constitution, or the Constitution of the United States, are void, and the Judiciary shall so declare them."

Experience has demonstrated that the difficulty with judicial review lies in the extent to which it is applied. In general, judges of both the federal and state courts have exercised restraint and sought to invalidate legislative acts only when they were clearly in conflict with constitutional provisions. But we do have examples of the abuse of judicial power. Thus, while the Constitution contained no provision on the subject, in *Dred Scott* vs. *Sandford* (1857) the Supreme Court ruled that Congress could not prohibit slavery in any territory of the United States and that the Compromise of 1850 was void. Abraham Lincoln expressed his contempt for this decision when in his first inaugural address he said: "The candid citizen must confess that if the policy of the government, upon vital questions affecting the whole people, is to be irrevocably fixed by decisions of the Supreme Court, the instant they are made, in ordinary litigation between parties in personal actions, the people will have ceased to be their own rulers, having to that extent practically resigned the government into the hands of that tribunal."

FRAMING A CONSTITUTION

The most widely used method for framing a constitution is for the state legislature to provide (a) for a constitutional convention, made up of representatives elected by the people, to write a constitution and (b) for the submission of the proposed new constitution to a vote by the people for ratification or rejection.

Georgia has had ten constitutions. Seven of them were written by conventions, but the Constitution of 1861 was the first to be submitted to a vote of the people. Comments are offered in the paragraphs that follow on the procedure used in writing Georgia's constitutions of 1945, 1976, and 1983.

CONSTITUTION OF 1945

Because of the abuse of power during the Reconstruction period, the framers of the Constitution of 1877, led by Robert Toombs, placed numerous restrictions upon the powers of government, particularly in the field of finance. As a result of the inclusion of numerous provisions statutory in nature, the document was amended 301 times in a period of sixty-eight years. Article VII alone, entitled "Finance, Taxation and Public Debt," was amended 188 times, but not more than fifteen percent of these amendments were of general interest, the greater number of them being applicable to a single city or county.

In March, 1943, the General Assembly passed a resolution, sponsored by Governor Ellis Arnall, providing for a commission of twenty-three members to revise the Constitution. The commission was to be composed of the Governor, the President of the Senate, the Speaker of the House of Representatives, three members of the Senate appointed by the President, five members of the House appointed by the Speaker, a justice of the Supreme Court designated by the Court, a judge of the Court of Appeals designated by the Court, the Attorney General, the State Auditor, two judges of the Superior Courts, three practicing attorneys-at-law, and three laymen appointed by the Governor. The resolution provided that the report of this commission should be submitted to the General Assembly either in the form of proposed amendments to the Constitution or as a proposed new Constitution, to be acted upon by the General Assembly and submitted to the people for ratification or rejection.

Pros and cons. There were two principal arguments in favor of the use of an appointed commission instead of an elected convention to revise the Constitution of Georgia. In the first place, the existing Constitution required a two-thirds vote of the total membership of both houses of the General Assembly to call a constitutional convention, and previous attempts to call a convention had failed. Since the work of the proposed commission would be submitted directly to the General Assembly and subjected to revision before submission to the people, the resolution creating it met with approval whereas a resolution calling a convention would probably have failed. Secondly, the preamble of the resolution authorizing the commission expressed the view that a revision of the Constitution could be accomplished "more satisfactorily by a small commission . . . than through a constitutional convention." A criticism advanced against the use of the appointed commission was that this method gave the incumbent administration too great an influence in shaping the fundamental law. Governor Arnall himself served as chairman of the commission and appointed eight of the other members; yet it should be noted that none of the ex officio members (the Attorney General, State Auditor, etc.) were appointed to their office by the Governor.

Work of the Commission. Fully ninety percent of the provisions of the Constitution of 1945 were taken from the amended Constitution of 1877. The work of the commission on revision was confined primarily to a revision of the form and organization of the document, albeit some of the changes in substance were of significance.

Adoption of Constitution. After extensive study and a number of revisions, the General Assembly approved the proposed new Constitution and submitted it to the people for ratification or rejection. At a special election held on August 7, 1945, the new Constitution was approved by a vote of 60,065 to 34,417.

COMMISSIONS OF 1963 AND 1969

The Constitution of 1945 continued most of the limitations on governmental power found in the Constitution of 1877. As a result, new constitutional amendments were proposed by every session of the General Assembly.

Commissions to revise the Constitution were appointed in 1963 and 1969. Both of these commissions wrote a new constitution, but neither of the documents was adopted. The federal district court in Atlanta enjoined the Secretary of State from submitting to the people the question of ratification of the Constitution written in 1964. The court held that a malapportioned legislature could not submit a new constitution to the people. The constitution written by the Commission of 1969 died in committee in the legislature.

CONSTITUTION OF 1976

The adoption of 75 amendments in 1972 brought to 767 the total number of amendments to the Constitution of 1945. Of these, 135 were amendments of state-wide application and 632 were local amendments, applicable to only one or more political subdivisions.

The need for constitutional revision was obvious. In 1973 leaders of the House of Representatives entrusted to the Office of Legislative Counsel the responsibility of rearranging and clarifying the substantive content of the Constitution. This office confined its work to rearranging the paragraphs and shifting them about. In 1975 the Judiciary Committee of the House made a few changes in the proposed draft, and in 1976 it was routinely passed by both the House and Senate. Submitted for ratification or rejection in the general election of November 2, 1976, the one-hundred and fifty page document was approved by a popular vote of 610,516 to 394, 734, by far the largest vote ever cast on any state constitution in Georgia.

CONSTITUTION OF 1983

The need for constitutional revision was not cured by the adoption of the Constitution of 1976, described by its supporters as an "editorial revision." The state Constitution remained excessively long and subject to numerous amendments at each biennial general election.

A 1977 resolution of the House of Representatives created an 11-member Select Committee on Constitutional Revision. It was composed of the Governor, Lieutenant Governor, Speaker of the House, President Pro Tem of the Senate, Speaker Pro Tem of the House, Chief Justice of the Supreme Court, Chief Judge of the Court of Appeals, Attorney General, Chairman of the Senate Judiciary Committee, Chairman of the House Judiciary Committee, and a trial judge appointed by the Judicial Council. This committee was to "act as the overall policy committee in directing and coordinating study and revision of the Constitution."

In 1979 Governor George Busbee appointed Pope B. McIntire as chairman of a 43-member State Bar Committee on the State Constitution. He also appointed Robin Harris, his former campaign manager, as executive director of the Select Committee on Constitutional Revision. Special committees were also appointed to work on separate articles of the Constitution.

In 1981 the General Assembly authorized a 60-member Legislative Overview Committee (30 Senators and 30 House members) to review the proposals of the various committees working on constitutional revision. This committee was to complete its work prior to the meeting of a special legislative session to consider the proposed new document.

The General Assembly met in special session on August 24, 1981, to deal with three subjects: (1) reapportionment of legislative districts, (2) revision of the statutory code, and (3) revision of the Constitution. It completed all three tasks and adjourned sine die on September 19.

In the general election of November 2, 1982, the proposed new Constitution was ratified by a vote of 567,663 to 211,342. The Constitution of 1983 is approximately a hundred pages long, but it is considerably shorter than the document which it replaced.

Analysis of the Constitution of 1983

The following statements, made without regard to the technicalities of legal phraseology and subject to the error inherent in all generalizations, point out the main provisions of the Constitution of 1983.

ARTICLE I

Bill of Rights

The Bill of Rights of the Constitution of Georgia includes all the guarantees of personal liberty found in the first eight amendments of the Constitution of the United States (freedom of religion, speech, press, etc.) and many others, among them a prohibition against banishment beyond the limits of the state or whipping as a punishment for crime. This long Bill of Rights dates from 1861. The earlier constitutions of Georgia had enumerated only four or five personal liberties. Thomas R. R. Cobb presented to the Convention of 1861 a 'Declaration of Fundamental Principles" embodying in twenty-eight paragraphs his conservative philosophy of government. This was adopted as Article I of the Constitution of 1861, and has been retained with minor alterations in subsequent constitutions.

Of the provisions of the Bill of Rights, the due process clause providing that "No person shall be deprived of life, liberty, or property except by due process of law," is most extensive in scope. In application it means that no person can be deprived of life, liberty, or property by any process which the judiciary considers unfair, arbitrary, or unreasonable.

The most satisfactory approach to understanding the meaning of any clause in the Bill of Rights is to study the decisions of the Supreme Court wherein the clause has been the subject of litigation. These decisions are published by the state under the title *Georgia Reports*, of which there were 250 volumes in 1982. Volume 2 of the *Georgia Code Annotated*, published by the Michie Company, contains citations to the leading cases. Another helpful tool in locating citations to the court decisions is the *Georgia Digest*, published in 23 volumes by the West Publishing Company.

ARTICLE II

Voting and Elections

To qualify to register to vote a person must be (1) a citizen of the United States, (2) a resident of the State of Georgia, and (3) 18 years old. No person can register who has (1) been convicted of a felony involving moral turpitude "except upon completion of the sentence," or (2) been judicially determined to be mentally incompetent "unless the disability has been removed."

"Elections by the people shall be by secret ballot and shall be conducted in accordance with procedures provided by law," states the Constitution. Detailed provisions governing both registration and voting procedure are contained in the *Georgia Election Code*, revised frequently and distributed by the Secretary of State.

ARTICLE III

The Legislative Branch

Legislative power is vested in a General Assembly, composed of a Senate and House of Representatives. The General Assembly is given power to make all laws deemed necessary and proper for the welfare of the state, provided they are not repugnant to the Constitution of Georgia or the laws of the United States.

THE SENATE

The Senate consists of not more than 56 members, each elected from a single-member district composed of contiguous territory. Senators are elected for two-year terms. The presiding officer of the Senate is the Lieutenant Governor.

THE HOUSE OF REPRESENTATIVES

The county was the traditional unit of representation in the House of Representatives. Under the Constitution of 1945, the 8 largest counties in population were given 3 representatives each, the 30 next largest counties were given 2 representatives each, and the remaining 121 counties were given 1 representative each. However, in the 1960s the United States Supreme Court applied a "one man one vote" rule requiring that representation in both houses of state legislatures be apportioned among legislative districts on the basis of population.

The Constitution of 1983 provides that the House of Representatives "shall consist of not fewer than 180 Representatives apportioned among representative districts of the State." The term of representatives is two years. The presiding officer of the house is called the Speaker.

SESSIONS

"The Senate and House of Representatives shall organize each odd-numbered year and shall be a different General Assembly for each two-year period. The General Assembly shall meet in regular session on the second Monday in January of each year, or otherwise as provided by law, and may continue in session for a period of no longer than 40 days in the aggregate each year. By concurrent resolution, the General Assembly may adjourn any regular session to such later date as it may fix for reconvening. Separate periods of adjournment may be fixed by one or more such concurrent resolutions."

The Governor is authorized to call special sessions of the General Assembly. Such a session is limited to 40 days, unless extended by a resolution passed by a three-fifth's vote in each house and approved by the Governor.

PRIVILEGES OF MEMBERS

"The members of both houses shall be free from arrest during sessions of the General Assembly, or committee meetings thereof, and in going thereto, or returning therefrom, except for treason, felony, larceny, or breach of the peace. No member shall be liable to answer in any other place for anything spoken in either house or in any committee meeting of either house."

POWERS OF EACH HOUSE

"Each house shall be the judge of the election, returns, and qualifications of its members, and shall have power to punish them for disorderly behavior or misconduct, by censure, fine, imprisonment, or expulsion; but no members shall be expelled, except by a vote of two-thirds of the members of the house to which such member belongs."

"Each house may punish by imprisonment, not extending beyond the session, any person not a member who shall be guilty of a contempt by any disorderly behavior in its presence or who shall rescue or attempt to rescue any person arrested by order of either house."

"A majority of the members to which each house is entitled shall constitute a quorum to transact business. A smaller number may adjourn from day to day and compel the presence of its absent members."

POWER OF THE GENERAL ASSEMBLY

The legislative power of the General Assembly is very broad. The General Assembly is not limited to powers expressed in the Constitution. It can pass all laws that it deems advisable that are not in conflict with the Constitution of the United States or the Constitution of Georgia. In theory the national government is limited to powers granted to it by the United States Constitution. This theory of "delegated powers" is not applicable to the government of the states of the American union. Thus it is meaningless to state in the Georgia Constitution that the General Assembly is authorized to tax to support public schools. The courts will assume that the General Assembly has such power unless there is a denial of it in the Constitution. Hence the most meaningful statements of state constitutions are negative statements (e.g., freedom of speech shall not be abridged), or positive statements that have negative implications (e.g., bills for raising revenue shall originate in the House of Representatives).

The procedure in enacting laws by the General Assembly of Georgia is in general similar to the procedure used in the Congress of the United States. In both cases, before becoming a law a bill must be passed by both houses of the legislature and approved by the chief executive, or passed over the executive veto by a two-thirds vote in both houses. As in Congress, each house of the General Assembly in Georgia has a number of standing committees to which bills are referred for study before being considered on the floor.

But while the procedure in enacting legislation in Georgia is in general similar to that in Congress, there are a number of significant differences. For example, in Georgia the vote of a majority of all members to which each house is entitled is necessary to pass a bill, whereas in Congress the requisite vote is a majority of the members *present;* and the Governor of Georgia may approve portions of an appropriation bill and disapprove other provisions, whereas the President of the United States must accept or reject a bill in its entirety.

APPROPRIATIONS CONTROLS

Each year in January when the General Assembly convenes in regular session, the Governor is directed to submit to it a budget report and a draft of a general appropriations bill for the next fiscal year. (The State's fiscal year begins on July 1. Funds appropriated to a State agency but not spent or contractually obligated by June 30 lapse.)

The General Assembly is prohibited from appropriating funds for any fiscal year in excess of the State funds already on hand plus the receipts anticipated to be collected, as estimated in the budget report submitted by the Governor.

Prior to 1945, several specific taxes were allocated to specific purposes. For example, taxes on alcoholic beverages were allocated to schools. Since 1945 the Constitution has provided that appropriations to State agencies "shall be for a specific sum of money, and no appropriation shall allocate to any object the proceeds of any particular tax or fund or a part or percentage thereof." A few exceptions are made, however. The Constitution itself appropriates for the maintenance of highways an amount each year equal to the previous year's receipts from motor fuel taxes.

IMPEACHMENT

"The House of Representatives shall have the sole power to vote impeachment charges against any executive or judicial officer of this state or any member of the General Assembly.

"The Senate shall have the sole power to try impeachments. When sitting for that purpose, the Senators shall be on oath, or affirmation, and shall be presided over by the Chief Justice of the Supreme Court. Should the Chief Justice be disqualified, then the Presiding Justice shall preside. Should the Presiding Justice be disqualified, then the Senate shall select a Justice of the Supreme Court to preside. No person shall be convicted without concurrence of two-thirds of the members to which the Senate is entitled.

"In cases of impeachment, judgments shall not extend further than removal from office and disqualification to hold and enjoy any office of honor, trust, or profit within this state or to receive a pension therefrom, but no such judgment shall relieve any party from any criminal or civil liability."

ARTICLE IV

Constitutional Boards and Commissions

A department headed by an individual has the advantage of concentrating authority; but some government agencies having the responsibility both to formulate and to execute policy are headed by a group of people. Several boards are provided for by the statutory law of Georgia; others are provided for in the Constitution. Article IV provides for six boards, as follows:

1. Public Service Commission (5 members; 6-year terms).
2. State Board of Pardons and Paroles (5 members; 7-year terms).
3. State Personnel Board (5 members; 5-year terms).
4. State Transportation Board (10 members; 5-year terms).
5. Veterans Service Board (7 members; 7-year terms).
6. Board of Natural Resources (15 members; 7-year terms).

The members of most of these boards are appointed by the Governor with confirmation by the Senate, and their terms are staggered in such a way as to give continuity to their personnel. Members of the Public Service Commission are elected by popular vote; members of the State Transportation Board are elected by the General Assembly.

The powers of the several boards are subject to varying degrees of control by the General Assembly.

ARTICLE V

Executive Branch

The Constitution vests "the chief executive power" in the Governor, and it is well to emphasize the importance of this office and who holds it.

ELECTION OF GOVERNOR

The Governor and other officers chosen on a state-wide basis are elected by a majority of the popular vote cast in an election held quadrennially (1986, 1990, etc.) on Tuesday after the first Monday in November. This date was chosen to coincide with the date of the election of members of Congress, who are elected every two years. Every four years presidential electors are also elected on this same day of the year; but, since presidential elections come in years divisible by four, it should be noted that Governors of Georgia and Presidents of the United States are not elected at the same time but at alternating two-year periods.

If no candidate for Governor receives a majority vote in the election, a run-off election is held between the two highest candidates. The same majority election rule applies to all state offices.

Term. The Governor is elected for a four-year term. "Persons holding the office of Governor may succeed themselves for one four-year term of office. Persons who have held the office of Governor and have succeeded themselves as hereinbefore provided shall not again be eligible to be elected to that office until after the expiration of four years from the conclusion of their term as Governor."

Succession. The Constitution provides for a Lieutenant Governor. He is elected at the same time and in the same manner as the Governor, and must have the same qualifications. The Lieutenant Governor is President of the Senate. In the event of the death, resignation, or permanent disability of the Governor, the Lieutenant Governor becomes Governor until the next general election for members of the General Assembly, when a Governor will be elected for the unexpired term. "If such death, resignation, or permanent disability shall occur within 30 days of the next general election or if the term will expire within 90 days after the next general election, the Lieutenant Governor shall become Governor for the unexpired term."

In case of the death, resignation, or disability of both the Governor and the Lieutenant Governor, succession passes to the Speaker of the House of Representatives. He shall exercise the executive power until a Governor, to be elected in a special election held within 90 days, shall qualify.

POWERS OF GOVERNOR

The Governor of Georgia has powers comparable to those of the governors of the other states of the American union. The Georgia Constitution vests "the chief executive power" in the Governor, but does not define this phrase. In practice, the Governor exercises a weighty influence in the government of the state. The campaign pledges of a successful candidate for Governor are likely to be enacted into law by the first session of the General Assembly convening after his inauguration. Under the state's statutory law, the Governor is named Director of the Budget and vested with extensive control over the finances of the state.

The Constitution lists a number of specific powers of the Governor. For example, the Governor "shall take care that the laws are faithfully executed," and he can "require information in writing from constitutional officers and all other officers and employees of the executive branch on any subject relating to the duties of their respective offices or employment."

Appointments and removals. The Governor's powers of appointment are important but, as is true in most of the states, those constitutional executive officers who are comparable to members of the President's cabinet in our national government are elected by popular vote. The Governor appoints the members of half a dozen constitutional boards and several hundred statutory officers. He also fills vacancies caused by the death or resignation of either judicial or executive officers, unless otherwise provided by law. Most of the major appointments require Senatorial confirmation.

The Governor's removal power is not nearly so extensive by comparison as that of the President of the United States. The Supreme Court of Georgia has repeatedly ruled that the Governor has no inherent power of removal. Hence in order to determine whether a particular officer is subject to removal by the Governor, and under what circumstances, it is necessary to consult the statutory law governing the office. In general, officials elected or appointed for a definite term are not subject to removal, but officials appointed for an indefinite term hold office at the pleasure of the Governor. In some instances the Governor is authorized to suspend an officer until the next meeting of the General Assembly, which may order the suspended official to be either removed or reinstated.

OTHER ELECTED EXECUTIVE OFFICERS

Other executive officers named in the Constitution and elected at the same time and in the same manner as the Governor and Lieutenant Governor are the (1) Attorney General, (2) Commissioner of Agriculture, (3) Commissioner of Insurance, (4) Commissioner of Labor, (5) Secretary of State, and (6) State School Superintendent.

DISABILITY

The Constitution states a procedure for determining whether an elected constitutional executive officer, including the Governor, "is unable to perform the duties of office because of a physical or mental disability." A petition for such a determination may be filed with the Supreme Court of Georgia by any four elected constitutional executive officers. After notice and hearing, the court shall decide the question. It is authorized to declare an office vacant if it finds the incumbent to be permanently disabled.

ARTICLE VI

The Judiciary

The Supreme Court and the Court of Appeals are courts of appellate jurisdiction only. The Superior Courts, which meet in every county, are the principal trial courts. There are, however, a number of other trial courts, some of which have specialized jurisdiction.

SUPREME COURT

The Supreme Court of Georgia is the state's highest court. Its decisions are binding as precedents on all other courts. The Court consists of "not more than nine Justices," elected for six-year terms. It has no original jurisdiction. It is a court for the correction of errors made by trial courts.

The Constitution provides that the Supreme Court shall exercise "exclusive appellate jurisdiction" in the following cases:

1. All cases involving the construction of a treaty or of the Constitution of the State of Georgia or of the United States and all cases in which the constitutionality of a law, ordinance, or constitutional provision has been drawn in question.
2. All cases of election contest.

The Supreme Court also has appellate jurisdiction over the following types of cases (unless otherwise provided by law):

1. Cases involving title to land.
2. All equity cases.
3. All cases involving wills.
4. All habeas corpus cases.
5. All cases involving extraordinary remedies.
6. All divorce and alimony cases.
7. All cases certified to it by the Court of Appeals.
8. All cases in which a sentence of death was imposed or could be imposed.

The Constitution specifically authorizes the Supreme Court to "review by certiorari cases in the Court of Appeals which are of gravity or great public importance."

COURT OF APPEALS

The Court of Appeals is composed of nine judges elected by popular vote for terms of six years. The court has no original jurisdiction. It was created to aid the Supreme Court in handling the many cases appealed from the trial courts. The Court of Appeals has appellate jurisdiction over "all cases not reserved to the Supreme Court or conferred on other courts by law." The judges of the Court of Appeals elect one of their members as Chief Judge, and he divides the members into three divisions of three judges each for hearing cases. If there is a dissent among the three judges in the decision of a case, the case is then heard by a full bench of nine judges.

SUPERIOR COURTS

The state is divided by statute into 43 superior court judicial circuits, with one or more judges in each. Judges of the Superior Courts are elected by the people for terms of four years. The judge of a Superior Court must hold court in every county within his circuit at least twice a year. The Superior Courts are the principal state courts of original jurisdiction for both criminal and civil cases, and have exclusive jurisdiction in (a) cases of divorce, (b) felony cases (except in the case of juvenile offenders), (c) cases respecting titles to land, and (d) equity cases. By statute the Superior Court of each county is given appellate jurisdiction over most cases tried by other courts in the county.

There is a District Attorney for each judicial circuit, elected in the same manner and for the same term as the judges of the Superior Courts, to represent the state in cases before the Superior Court. In each county a sheriff enforces orders of the Superior Court and a clerk keeps its records.

PROBATE COURTS

The Constitution establishes a Probate Court for each county. The judge of this court is elected for a term of four years. The jurisdiction of the Probate Court, fixed by statute, covers the probation of wills, administration of estates, appointment of guardians, and the issuance of lunacy commissions. Appeals from decisions of the Probate Court are taken to the Superior Court of the county.

STATE COURTS OF COUNTIES

Under the Constitution of 1877, appeals from inferior courts could be made to the Superior Court of the county, but not to the Supreme Court or to the Court of Appeals. Only decisions by a Superior Court or by a "City Court" (meeting designated specifications) could be appealed directly to one of the state's two appellate courts. Through the years 60-odd city courts with the designated specifications were created by special acts. The name "city court" was misleading since a court of this type had county-wide jurisdiction, for example, the City Court of Athens in and for Clarke County.

An act of 1970 changed the name of these courts to the State Court of (name of county in which the court is located) County. The act applies to "all courts in this State that are below the level of superior courts and have concurrent jurisdiction with superior courts to try misdemeanor cases by a jury trial or have civil jurisdiction unlimited in amount and concurrent with the superior courts in all matters, except those matters which are vested exclusively in the superior courts or have both of the above jurisdictions." In 1982 there were 60 such courts.

MAGISTRATE COURT

The name Justice of the Peace Court was changed to Magistrate Court by the Constitution of 1983.

From colonial days to the present, justices of the peace have been available throughout Georgia to settle minor cases. The smallest political district of the state is the militia district, numbering 1,726 in 1980. Prior to 1983 there was a justice of the peace for most militia districts, elected by the people of the district for a term of four years. In some metropolitan areas, however, justice courts had been replaced by other systems of courts.

The Constitution provides that "justice of the peace courts, small claims courts, and magistrate courts operating on the effective date of this Constitution (July 1, 1983) and the County Court of Echols County shall become and be classified as magistrate courts." It also provides that magistrate courts "shall have uniform jurisdiction as provided by law."

JUVENILE COURTS

Since 1915 a number of special acts and several general laws have provided for juvenile courts. The Juvenile Court Act of 1951 created juvenile courts for counties having a population of 50,000 or more, continued existing juvenile courts in smaller counties, and authorized the creation of a juvenile court in any county upon the recommendation of two successive grand juries. In counties not having a juvenile court, the judge of the Superior Court was authorized to act as a juvenile court judge. Juvenile courts were given jurisdiction over children under 17 years of age charged with crime.

Under existing statutory law, the judge of a juvenile court for any county is appointed by the judge or judges of the Superior Court of the circuit in which the county is located. He in turn appoints probation officers, employees of detention homes, and other needed personnel.

The Constitution of 1983 provides that "Juvenile courts shall continue as juvenile courts" and "shall have uniform jurisdiction as provided by law."

ARTICLE VII

Taxation and Finance

"The state may not suspend or irrevocably give, grant, limit, or restrain the right of taxation, and all . . . acts to effect any of these purposes are null and void," states the Constitution. There are some old contracts granting perpetual tax exemptions, notably the 1833 charter of the Georgia Railroad and Banking Company, but no more such contracts can be made.

PROPERTY TAX LIMITED

The State of Georgia receives most of its income from a general sales tax of 3 percent; special sales taxes on motor fuel, alcoholic beverages, and other specific products; and income taxes. The Constitution limits the state tax levy on tangible property for any one year to one-fourth mill on each dollar of the value of the property. Thus the state tax on a house and lot valued at $30,000 cannot exceed $7.50 per year. (The tax rate by cities and counties is another story!)

EXEMPTIONS FROM TAXATION

The Constitution authorizes any county or municipality to exempt from ad valorem taxes two types of property: (a) "Inventories of goods in the process of manufacture or production, and inventories of finished goods," and (b) "tangible property used in a solar energy heating or cooling system" and machinery used in the manufacture of such systems. An exemption for inventories must be approved in a referendum.

Other than inventories and solar equipment, the Constitution of 1983 does not list the types of property to be exempted from taxation. Instead, it converts the former constitutional provisions on the subject into "statutory law until otherwise provided by law."

In general, a bill creating a new tax exemption must be approved by a two-thirds vote in both houses of the General Assembly and by a majority vote in a statewide referendum. However, homestead exemptions from local taxes may be authorized by local legislation, approved in a local referendum.

In general, the Constitution does not set a two-thirds vote or any other special requirement limiting the power of the General Assembly to repeal or reduce an exemption from taxation. However, there are two exceptions: (a) any bill which repeals or reduces a homestead exemption must pass each house by a two-thirds vote and be approved in a referendum, and (b) a bill which reduces or repeals exemptions on burial grounds or institutions of purely public charity must receive a two-thirds vote in each house.

STATE DEBT

Close restrictions were placed upon the power of the State to incur debts by the Constitution of 1877. By 1947 the State of Georgia was debt free.

The constitutional limitations on State debts were circumvented in a wholesale manner during the 1950s and 1960s. The legislature created public corporations, usually called "authorities." These authorities issued bonds to raise money to build public facilities. The facilities were then leased to State departments. Funds paid by State departments under lease contracts were used to amortize authority-bonds. For example, the State School Building Authority created in 1951 issued bonds and financed the construction of school buildings. These buildings were leased to public schools under contracts which provided for annual rental payments for a number of years, after which time the school buildings should become the property of the school systems formerly holding them by lease.

Public corporations created included the Hospital Authority

(1939), State Park Authority (1941), Ports Authority (1945), University Building Authority (1949), Jekyll Island State Park Authority (1950), State School Building Authority (1951), State Office Building Authority (1951), State Bridge Building Authority (1953), Rural Road Authority (1955), Farmers Market Authority (1955), Stone Mountain Memorial Association (1958), and Penal and Rehabilitation Authority (1960).

The Georgia Supreme Court sustained the public corporations ("authorities") system of financing public facilities. In *McLucas* vs. *State Bridge Building Authority* (1953) the opinion read: "While the Authority is an instrument of the State, it is nevertheless not the State . . . nor an agency of the State. It is a mere creature of the State, having distinct corporate entity. . . . Its revenue bonds . . . are not . . . debts of the State. . . ."

By 1962 the indebtedness of Georgia's public authorities exceeded $400 million. To aid in the further sale of bonds by these authorities, the State Constitution was amended that year by adding a guarantee that the State would appropriate funds to meet obligations arising under lease contracts between state agencies and public authorities. In 1967 State control over public authorities was expanded and the names of several of the existing authorities changed.

Finally, in 1972, the pretense that the State could not incur bonded debt was dropped. A constitutional amendment of that year authorized the State both to incur general obligation debt and to incur debt by guaranteeing the payment of revenue obligations issued for designated purposes by State instrumentalities. A debt of either type must be approved in advance by the General Assembly. The Constitution places a 10 percent limit on State debt. No new debt can be incurred at any time when the amount of the annual payments owed by State agencies under existing debts (including obligations arising under lease contracts) exceeds 10 percent of the State's revenue in the immediately preceding fiscal year.

ARTICLE VIII

Education

"The provision of an adequate public education for the citizens shall be a primary obligation of the State of Georgia. Public education for the citizens prior to the college or postsecondary level shall be free and shall be provided for by taxation." Thus reads the first two sentences of Article VIII.

STATE BOARD OF EDUCATION

General control over public education below college level has long been vested in the State Board of Education. This board is now composed of one member from each of the ten congressional districts of the state. Members are appointed by the Governor, with senatorial confirmation, for periods of seven years. The Constitution states that the board "shall have such powers and duties as provided by law."

State School Superintendent. The executive officer of the State Board of Education is the State School Superintendent. He is elected by popular vote for a term of four years.

BOARD OF REGENTS

In 1930 Georgia had 27 boards of trustees of separate state-supported colleges. The Reorganization Act of 1931 sponsored by Governor Richard B. Russell, Jr., abolished these separate boards and concentrated control over state institutions of higher education in one Board of Regents.

There are 15 members on the Board of Regents—one from each congressional district in the state and five additional members from the state-at-large. All members are appointed by the Governor with senatorial confirmation for terms of seven years.

The Board of Regents was made a constitutional board in 1943 as a means of giving it protection against political interference. The Constitution of 1983 contains several paragraphs on the powers of the Board of Regents, including the following:

"The board of regents shall have the exclusive authority to create new public colleges, junior colleges, and universities in the State of Georgia, subject to approval by majority vote in the House of Representatives and the Senate. Such vote shall not be required to change the status of a college, institution or university existing on the effective date of this Constitution. The government, control, and management of the University System of Georgia and all of the institutions in said system shall be vested in the Board of Regents of the University System of Georgia.

"All appropriations made for the use of any or all institutions in the university system shall be paid to the board of regents in a lump sum, with the power and authority in said board to allocate and distribute the same among the institutions under its control in such way and manner and in such amounts as will further an efficient and economical administration of the university system."

In practice the Board of Regents extends a great amount of

autonomy to the local units of the University System of Georgia. In 1982 there were 33 units, as follows:

Abraham Baldwin Agricultural College
Tifton

Albany Junior College
Albany

Albany State College
Albany

Armstrong State College
Savannah

Atlanta Junior College
Atlanta

Augusta College
Augusta

Bainbridge Junior College
Bainbridge

Brunswick Junior College
Brunswick

Clayton Junior College
Morrow

Columbus College
Columbus

Dalton Junior College
Dalton

Emanuel County Junior College
Swainsboro

Floyd Junior College
Rome

Fort Valley State College
Fort Valley

Gainesville Junior College
Gainesville

Georgia College
Milledgeville

Georgia Institute of Technology
Atlanta

Georgia Southern College
Statesboro

Georgia Southwestern College
Americus

Georgia State University
Atlanta

Gordon Junior College
Barnesville

Kennesaw College
Marietta

Macon Junior College
Macon

Medical College of Georgia
Augusta

Middle Georgia College
Cochran

North Georgia College
Dahlonega

Savannah State College
Savannah

South Georgia College
Douglas

Southern Technical Institute
Marietta

University of Georgia
Athens

Valdosta State College
Valdosta

Waycross Junior College
Waycross

West Georgia College
Carrollton

LOCAL SCHOOL DISTRICTS

The county has always been the basic administrative unit for public schools in Georgia. However, about two-dozen cities operate their schools independent of the county board of education. There are also a few area school districts (formed by consolidation) which operate directly under the State Board of Education. Each local school system has a board of education and a school superintendent. The superintendent is the executive officer of the board.

Funds for public schools are provided by the federal government, by the state, and by local governments. The Georgia Constitution places limitations on local taxes for education.

"The board of education of each school system shall annually certify to its fiscal authority or authorities a school tax not greater than 20 mills per dollar for the support and maintenance of education." The amount of tax "certified" by a board of education is binding upon the fiscal authorities of the county.

The 20 mill limit on school taxes does not apply uniformly throughout the state. The limit may be increased or decreased in any school district by action of the local board of education, approved in a popular referendum.

ARTICLE IX

Counties and Municipalities

Georgia is divided into 159 counties which are, on the one hand, administrative divisions of the state, and, on the other, corporate bodies vested by law with certain powers of their own. No additional counties can be created.

"The General Assembly may provide by law for the consolidation of two or more counties into one or the division of a county and the merger of portions thereof into other counties under such terms and conditions as it may prescribe; but no such consolidation, division, or merger shall become effective unless approved by a majority of the qualified voters voting thereon in each of the counties proposed to be consolidated, divided, or merged." Three counties, Milton, Campbell, and Fulton, were consolidated into one in 1931.

The General Assembly is also specifically authorized to provide consolidated government for cities and counties, subject to approval by referendum. A unified government was approved for Muscogee County and the City of Columbus in 1970.

COUNTY COMMISSIONERS

The Constitutions of 1877, 1945, and 1976 all authorized the General Assembly to create county commissioners "in such counties as may require them." The Constitution of 1983 does not specifically mention county commissioners; however, it provides that the "governing authorities of the several counties shall remain as prescribed by law on June 30, 1983, until otherwise provided by law." The governing authority in 156 counties is the Board of Commissioners, which has control of taxation, roads, public buildings, paupers, and other county matters. In Towns and Union counties these powers are exercised by the Probate Court, and in Muscogee County there is a council for the consolidated Muscogee-City of Columbus government. The county commissioners for the several counties vary in number from one to nine, but most counties have either three or five commissioners. Most of them are elected, but in a few counties they are appointed by the grand jury.

OTHER COUNTY OFFICERS

The Constitution lists only six county officers: judge of the probate court, clerk of the superior court, sheriff, tax receiver, tax collector, and tax commissioner "where such office has replaced the tax receiver and tax collector." They are to be elected for terms of four years.

HOME RULE

The term "home rule" is not clearly defined, but in general it means a large amount of local self-government. The Constitution authorizes the General Assembly to grant home rule to cities and counties, but in practice much local legislation is enacted by the General Assembly itself. The statutes enacted by the General Assembly are published annually as *Georgia Laws* in two volumes. Volume I contains laws of state-wide application. Volume II, usually several thousand pages long, contains laws of local application.

DEBT LIMITS

The debt that may be incurred by a county, city, or other political subdivision is limited to 10 percent of the assessed value of the taxable property therein. Any new debt (except a temporary loan to supply a casual deficiency) must be approved in a referendum.

Revenue anticipation obligations may be issued by a county, city, or other political subdivision to provide funds for revenue-producing facilities, including gas or electric generating systems. Such obligations are not construed to be debts within the meaning of the constitutional debt limitation.

ARTICLE X

Amendments to the Constitution

The first two paragraphs of this article read as follows:

"Amendments to this Constitution or a new Constitution may be proposed by the General Assembly or by a constitutional convention, as provided in this article. Only amendments which are of general and uniform applicability throughout the state shall be proposed, passed, or submitted to the people.

"A proposal by the General Assembly to amend this Constitution or to provide for a new Constitution shall originate as a resolution in either the Senate or the House of Representatives and, if approved by two-thirds of the members to which each house is entitled in a roll-call vote entered on their respective journals, shall be submitted to the electors of the entire state at the next general election which is held in the even-numbered years. A summary of such proposal shall be prepared by the Attorney General, the Legislative Counsel, and the Secretary of State and shall be published in the official organ of each county and, if deemed advisable by the 'Constitutional Amendments Publication Board,' in not more than 20 other newspapers in the state designated by such board which meet the qualifications for being selected as the official organ of a county. Said board shall be composed of the Governor, the Lieutenant Governor, and the Speaker of the House of Representatives. Such summary shall be published once each week for three consecutive weeks immediately preceding the day of the general election at which such proposal is to be submitted. The language to be used in submitting a proposed amendment or a new Constitution shall be in such words as the General Assembly may provide in the resolution or, in the absence thereof, in such language as the Governor may prescribe. A copy of the entire proposed amendment or of a new Constitution shall be filed in the office of the judge of the probate court of each county and shall be available for public inspection; and the summary of the proposal shall so indicate. The General Assembly is hereby authorized to provide by law for additional matters relative to the publication and distribution of proposed amendments and summaries not in conflict with the provisions of this Paragraph."

To become effective a constitutional amendment proposed by the General Assembly must be approved by a majority vote of the electors voting thereon in the general election at which the amendment is submitted for ratification.

The Constitution provides an additional method for use either in proposing amendments or in proposing a new constitution, namely, the use of a constitutional convention. The provision on this subject reads as follows:

"No convention of the people shall be called by the General Assembly to amend this Constitution or to propose a new Constitution, unless by the concurrence of two-thirds of the members to which each house of the General Assembly is entitled. The representation in said convention shall be based on population as near as practicable. A proposal by the convention to amend this Constitution or for a new Constitution shall be advertised, submitted to, and ratified by the people in the same manner provided for advertisement, submission, and ratification of proposals to amend the Constitution by the General Assembly. The General Assembly is hereby authorized to provide the procedure by which a convention is to be called and under which such convention shall operate and for other matters relative to such constitutional convention."

ARTICLE XI

Miscellaneous

This concluding article deals with a number of technical matters, including the continuation of present officers and laws. Under its terms, many of the local amendments to the Constitutions of 1877, 1945, and 1976 will not continue as part of the State Constitution after July 1, 1987, unless specified measures are taken to preserve them.

Questions on the Constitution of Georgia

PART I

History and Fundamental Principles

1. Give a general account of the constitution history of Georgia, including the dates of the adoption of new constitutions.
2. Explain fully the meaning of "constitutional government," including a distinction between constitutional law and statutory law.
3. Explain the principle of "the separation of powers" and "checks and balances," including illustrations.
4. Explain the meaning of "judicial review."
5. Write an essay on the method used in framing the Constitution of 1945, showing how this method differed from the conventional method of framing constitutions, and evaluating the merits of the procedure.
6. Write a critical essay on the Constitution of Georgia, pointing out its strengths and weaknesses and proposing such changes as you consider desirable.

PART II

The Constitution as an Objective Document

I. Bill of Rights
   1. What purpose is served by a bill of rights?
   2. List several provisions of the Bill of Rights and comment upon their meaning.

II. Elective Franchise
   1. Who can vote in Georgia? Explain the procedure for registration.

III. Legislative Branch
   1. How many members are there in the General Assembly?
   2. What is the basis of the apportionment of representation in the House? In the Senate?
   3. What is the term of representatives? Of Senators?
   4. How often are sessions of the General Assembly held, and how long does a session last?

5. State the provisions made for special sessions of the General Assembly.
6. Discuss the privileges of members of the General Assembly.
7. Name the principal officers of both the Senate and the House of Representatives.
8. What difference is there between the vote necessary to pass a bill in the General Assembly of Georgia and the vote necessary to pass a bill in Congress?
9. Describe the process of impeachment.
10. How broad is the power of the General Assembly?
11. What appropriation controls are set forth in the Constitution? When does a general appropriation bill expire?

IV. Constitutional Boards and Commissions

1. What purposes are served by providing for boards and commissions in the Constitution?
2. Give the composition of as many of the constitutional boards and commissions as you can.

V. Executive Branch

1. Tell how the Governor of Georgia is elected.
2. Can a Governor be reelected?
3. What is the line of succession to the office of Governor?
4. Compare the appointing and removal power of the Governor to that of the President of the United States.
5. Does the Governor have a broad removal power?
6. List the eight executive officers named in the Constitution.
7. What is the procedure for determining the disability of a constitutional executive officer?

VI. Judiciary

1. Give the composition and the jurisdiction of both the Supreme Court and the Court of Appeals.
2. Describe the Superior Courts and their jurisdiction.
3. How many Probate Courts are there in Georgia? What do they do?
4. Can a case be appealed to the State Court of Appeals from a State Court (at the county level)?
5. How many Magistrate Courts are there in Georgia? What is their function?

VII. Taxation and Finance

1. What limit is placed upon State property taxes?
2. Summarize the limitations on State debts.

VIII. Education

1. Give the composition of each of the following: (1) State

Board of Education, (2) Board of Regents, (3) County Board of Education.
2. Explain the provisions on local school taxes.

IX. Counties and Municipalities
1. Explain the legal status of a county.
2. How many counties are there in Georgia? How could this number be reduced?
3. List the county officers named in the Constitution and comment upon the function of each. How are they chosen? For what term?
4. What is the limit upon debts by cities and counties?

X. Amendments
1. How can the Constitution be amended?

XI. Miscellaneous
1. Are local constitutional amendments adopted under former state constitutions continued in effect under the Constitution of 1983?

Bibliography

Chart of Georgia State Government, revised periodically and published by the Institute of Government, University of Georgia, Athens, Ga.

The Code of Georgia, available in multivolume annotated edition, revised frequently and sold by the Michie Company of Charlottesville, Va.

Coleman, Kenneth, et al., *A History of Georgia*. Athens: University of Georgia Press, 1977.

Coulter, E. Merton, *Georgia, A Short History*. Chapel Hill: University of North Carolina Press, 1947.

Georgia Election Code, revised frequently and distributed by the office of the Secretary of State, State Capitol, Atlanta, Ga.

Georgia Official Directory of State and County Officers, revised frequently and distributed by the Secretary of State.

Georgia Statistical Abstract, revised frequently and distributed by the Bureau of Business Research, University of Georgia, Athens, Ga.

Gibson, Frank and T. L. Hammock, *Forms of City Government in Georgia*. Institute of Government, University of Georgia. 1957.

Jackson, Edwin L., *Handbook for Legislators*. Athens: Institute of Government, 1976.

———, *Handbook of Georgia State Agencies*. Athens: Institute of Government, 1975.

Saye, Albert B., *A Constitutional History of Georgia*. Athens: University of Georgia Press, 1970.

———, *Georgia History and Government*. Austin: Steck-Vaughn Co., 1981.